D0909838

LYING: A Critical Analysis

LYING: A Critical Analysis

Warren Shibles
UNIVERSITY OF WISCONSIN-WHITEWATER

THE LANGUAGE PRESS
P.O. BOX 342 WHITEWATER, WISCONSIN 53190 U.S.A.

ISBN 0-912386-20-7
LC 85-80835

All books below are by the same author:

Published by the Language Press:

TEACHING YOUNG PEOPLE TO BE CRITICAL SERIES:

Good and Bad are Funny Things: A Rhyming Book (Ethics for Children) 1978
Ethics for Children, 1978
Emotions: A Critical Analysis for Children, 1978
Humor: A Critical Analysis for Young People, 1978
Time: A Critical Analysis for Children, 1978

BOOKS FOR PROFESSIONALS AND ADULTS

Rational Love, 1978
Humor: A Comprehensive Classification and Analysis, 1978
Wittgenstein, Language and Philosophy, 1970
Death: An Interdisciplinary Analysis, 1974
Emotion, 1974
Metaphor: An Annotated Bibliography and History, 1971
Essays on Metaphor, 1972
An Analysis of Metaphor, 1971 (Distributed by The Language Press, Published by Mouton, Netherlands)
Philosophical Pictures, 1971

OTHER PUBLISHERS

Models of Ancient Greek Philosophy (Vision, England) 1971
Wittgenstein, Sprache und Philosophie (Bouvier, Bonn) 1973
Philosophische Bilder (Bouvier, Bonn) 1973
Wittgenstein, Linguagem E Filosofia (Editoria Cultrix Brazil) 1974
Emootiot. Lohja, Finland: Julkaisija 1979
Etiikkaa. Lohja, Finland: Julkaisija 1979
Wittgenstein, Lengua y filosofia (Universidad Veracruzana, Mexico) 1985

Printed in the United States of America

for Carolyn, one of the most honest people I know.

I DO BELIEVE HER THOUGH I KNOW SHE LIES. I LIE WITH HER AND SHE WITH ME AND IN OUR FAULTS BY LIES WE FLATTERED BE. SELF-LIE: TO BELIEVE WHAT WE DO NOT BELIEVE DOES NOT EXHILARATE. BELIEF MEANS NOT WANTING TO KNOW WHAT IS TRUE. I AM THAT WHICH MUST ALWAYS OVERCOME ITSELF. THE WORST ENEMY YOU CAN ENCOUNTER WILL ALWAYS BE YOURSELF. YOU LIE IN WAIT FOR YOURSELF IN CAVES AND WOODS. WE BELIEVE IN FICTIONS, LIFE-LIES, IMPOSSIBLE THINGS SUCH AS THAT TIME IS AN ENTITY, SPACE IS AN INVISIBLE FLUID, AND THAT MIND IS A GHOST WHICH HAUNTS THE BODY. LIES ARE LIKE GLOW WORMS. THEY REQUIRE DARKNESS TO GLOW IN. LIES ARE IMAGINARY GARDENS WITH REAL PEOPLE IN THEM.

TABLE OF CONTENTS

"Pretty much all the honest truth telling there is in the world is done by children."

Supreme Court Justice
Oliver Wendell Holmes

"Lying is a language-game that needs to be learned like any other one."

Ludwig Wittgenstein
Philosophical Investigations, #249
(Note 1)

"Most of all, Wittgenstein tried to infuse in students a devotion to honesty."

Professor William Bartley III

"The big lie is more plausible than truth."

Ernest Hemingway

"Omnis homo mendax" (all people lie)

Psalms

"Lying about what I see . . . is knowing what I see and saying something else."

Wittgenstein (1968 p. 280)

PREFACE

This book is written so that it may be understood not only by scholars and adults, but by young people as well. The technical material for scholars is placed in the "Notes" at the end of the book.

The book is especially valuable for teachers as a resource tool or as a text for use in classes. Exercises have been added for this purpose. The issues involved go far beyond the clarification of the word "lying." In this respect, to clarify lying is to clarify thinking in general.

Not to be interested in critical thinking, or philosophy, is to "fake" life. It is a life-lie. The person who is not interested in philosophy, is not interested in life.

I wish to especially thank Dr. Gabriel Falkenberg of the University of Düsseldorf, Dr. David Cartwright, Dr. Arno Plack of Heidelberg, and Prof. Gershon Weiler for reading and offering suggestions regarding the manuscript.

Dr. Albert Ellis, Executive Director of the Institute for Rational Therapy, was also kind enough to read the manuscript giving the following analysis:

> I found it an unusual, perceptive and complete analysis of lying and one I have not come across elsewhere. I think it is a very valuable addition to the literature and brings together many points not made in other works.

An Introduction by Gabriel Falkenberg*

Language doesn't lie, people do. They do it by using language. What is lying? And what in the structure of language and communication makes lying and deceiving possible?

The beginning of one answer is surely that what people say can diverge from *what they think,* or believe: linguistic appearance need not conform to the psychological reality behind it. Speech can be like a mask. Statements may be truthful, or untruthful.

A second answer has been that what people say can diverge from *how things are:* linguistic representation need not conform to the reality out there. Speech can be like a misleading signpost. Statements may be true, or false.

*Dr. Gabriel Falkenberg. Author of: *Ansätze zu einer Theorie der Lüge* Dissertation. Universität Düsseldorf 1978; *Lügen: Grundzüge einer Theorie sprachlicher Täuschung* Tübingen: Max Niemeyer 1982.

Simply to stick to the second answer cannot be sufficient: if people say something that is false, that may well be an error rather than a lie. It has also been suggested - first by Augustine, the first great analyst of the lie - that falsity is not even necesary: One may even lie by saying the truth.

Neither is the first answer satisfactory as it stands: if people say something that they do not believe, that may well be irony, wit or exaggeration, rather than a lie.

Speech is neither a mirror of the "thought inside," nor a mirror of the world outside. Any analysis of lying has, therefore, to pay attention to both answers, to the partial "thought"-independency as well as to the partial world-independency of speech, while keeping sight of the dangers of a sterile representationalism at the one extreme, and of a free-floating mentalism at the other.

In order to capture the essence of the lie, additional requirements would have to be added to both of the two answers mentioned, requirements such as knowledge or belief that the statement is false, or the intention to deceive. A minimal requirement for any account would be the following: lying is using language in order to produce error, in order to generate beliefs other than those that one really holds.

Acts of lying are linguistic acts; but their description has to mention the beliefs and intentions of the liar. Thus, any account of lying has to deal with those psychological concepts.

When someone tells us something, e.g., that the sun is shining outside, what does it mean for us to believe her or him? What is it to form the belief that the sun is shining, on the basis of this statement? (Suppose we have no possibility to go and see for ourselves.) It seems as though we have to suppose that the speaker is *truthful* (believes what is told us) and is *competent* (not erroneous in this belief). Put crudely: from the fact that someone has *said* that such-and-such, we derive the fact that it *is really* so by supposing that the speaker *believes* that such-and-such and that such belief is correct.

This is what is meant by the truism that communication is impossible without a minimum of trust and reliability. (Imagine a group of inveterate liars: could it count as a society?) The successful liar sabotages the interpersonal process of information-transmission by leading others into error as to his real beliefs, and thus leading them (if he is not himself in error) into error as to the real world. He may even, if that is conceivable, effectively lie to himself.

The lie is therefore parasitic on the social process: it depends for its success on credibility and reliability that it serves to undermine at the same moment. This destruction of trust, testimony and tradition is what many philosophers see as the main reason why lying is, in general, immoral.

The earliest moral condemnations of lying were indeed judicial laws against false witnesses and perjury, such as the famous roughly four thousand year old *Code of Hammurabi* which states at the outset: "If a citizen appears as a false witness in court . . ., he shall be put to death." The Ninth Commandment, traditionally given as "Thou shalt not lie," is also in its original form correctly to be translated as, "Thou shalt not give evidence as a lying witness against your fellow creature." (*Exodus* 20,16)

Not all languages, though, have a separate word for *lie*. Classical Greek is one example: there, "pseudos" can mean error, lie, fiction, mere appearance, and other things. One may speculate, with some justification, that this signifies a stage of human thought where attention to (what we call) objective matters, was predominant: what did matter was that someone said something false — whether consciously and intentionally or not, was of secondary importance. The clear, lexical distinction between the *factual* and the *personal* — e.g., in Latin the separation of "error" and "mendacium" (lie), later of "veritas" (truth) and "veracitas" (truthfulness) was no mean cultural achievement.

Today, an analysis of lying has to take into consideration the mutifarious lexical means with which lying and a host of related phenomena can be designated in modern language. Warren Shibles leads us, in his lively and practical book, into this fascinating area of human thought and language.

Language doesn't lie; people do. A computer can be programmed to give wrong answers. But what would it mean for a machine to lie? Maybe only creatures who possess the capability of lying can state something in the full-blooded sense. And perhaps only creatures who know that freedom includes the freedom to make errors and to be led into error, can value truth and truthfulness.

Gabriel Falkenberg May 1985

INTRODUCTION

"Lie" is a common and familiar word. Even in childhood we accept it like someone we have known for a long time. We think we know what it is about and how to deal with it.

It is a word like many others in our language, such as mind, idea, time, good, bad, love, spirit. Such words are as familiar as our own names. We think we know what they mean until we question them. Similarly, when we question "good" and "bad" we create the study of ethics, books on which could fill many libraries.

The problem with the word "lie" is that it is all too familiar. We must make it a stranger. We must put questions to it and become acquainted with it all over again. We must see how it lives and the kind of life it leads. The lie has its own language (e.g., fib, "white lie," perjury), its own people (e.g., liars, hypocrites, gossips), and its own world (life-lie). We will have to study this language, these people, this world. There are very few books about the lie. In this respect it will be an adventure into the practically unknown. Once this world is entered no one will return the same as before.

We are commonly told by those around us that we should never tell a lie. The philosopher Immanuel Kant believed that we should never in any case tell a lie. He said it is our duty never to lie no matter how harmful the results may be. But other philosophers (such as Jeremy Bentham and Henry Sidgwick) oppose Kant.[2] They believe that the consequences do determine whether or not we should tell a lie. We thus have contradictory views about lying.[3]

What if by telling a lie, we cause no harm, yet save the lives of many people? Perhaps in this case we should lie, and not merely follow duty blindly. But Kant said that we should, if asked, even reveal to a murderer the place of the person to be murdered. Some say we should not lie even to save our own lives.[4]

Also, we find that even those who say we should never lie, in fact, tell a great many lies. Sissela Bok, in her interesting book, **Lying** (1978), found that lying occurs among every profession.[5]

She wrote:

> Most doctors, in a number of surveys, stated that they do not, as a rule, inform patients that they have an illness such as cancer. (pp. 228, 229)
>
> Many lie to children and to those who are ill, about matters . . . quite central, such as birth, adoption, divorce, and death. Deceptive propaganda and misleading advertising abound. (p. 60)
>
> Some laws even require deception. (p. 245)

Niccolo Machiavelli (1469-1527), the statesman and political philosopher, wrote, "It is necessary to know how to disguise . . ., and to be a great pretender . . . ." He believed that it was necessary for the great ruler to lie.[3]

Something must be wrong with our common views about lying if they can be so easily shown to be false or harmful. Society is confused about what a lie is and whether or not we should ever lie.[6] We will attempt here to clarify lying and resolve its contradictions.

We need first to find out what a lie is. Then we will be able to determine such things as whether or not we should ever tell one.

I. The Dictionary Definition

Webster's Dictionary (1981) states that a lie is "to make an untrue statement with intent to deceive," and "an untrue or inaccurate statement that may or may not be believed by the speaker." "To deceive" means to cause someone to believe what is false.[7]

We will next examine this definition to see whether or not it is false.

A. Must a lie always be a false statement?

Examine these cases:

Case 1. A pupil says, "Paris is the capital of England." She believes this is true. Is she lying? What she says is false. But because she believes it is true, she is not lying. She is just wrong.

Thus, we can make false statements which are not lies. As observers, we cannot know if a statement is a lie merely by knowing that it is false.

Case 2. A pupil says, "He stole the money." He believes that is false, but it turns out to be true. *What* he says is true. But because he thought it was false he lied. Thus, we can lie by telling the truth. In this case, *we can lie and tell the truth at the same time!* There are two truths confessed here: (a) what we think is true, and (b) objective truth. The equivocation or double meaning here is truth (a) for us, or (b) for others. To say a lie is an untruth does not tell us whether we mean sense (a) or sense (b).

Thus, the dictionary definition is wrong. We can make a false statement, yet not lie (Case 1). And we can lie, yet tell the truth (Case 2). We cannot know if someone is lying merely by knowing the truth or falsity of a statement. Thus, a lie is not merely an untruth or false statement.

The dictionary definition also states that a lie is saying what is false in order to deceive someone.

B. Must a lie deceive in order to be a lie?

"To deceive" here means to intend for someone else to believe that the false statement is true.

Case 1. A criminal may force me to lie to a friend, but I may hope that my friend does not believe the lie. But we would say it is a lie whether or not we intend someone to believe it. We say the criminal forced us to lie. Thus, we may lie without wanting to mislead or deceive. Again, the dictionary definition is wrong.

Case 2. A fisherman says, "I caught a fish three miles long." This is said as a joke. He lied, but he knew no one would be misled or deceived. Again, it is a lie, but is not meant to deceive.

Case 3. Your younger brother carelessly painted part of the window glass when he painted the room. You say, "It is wonderful what you can do with just paint and a brush." That is, you did not say what you believed. You used irony. Your younger brother may or may not know if you like his painting job. The lie does not depend on whether or not the listener knows it is a lie. It is a lie anyway. So the dictionary definition is again wrong.

Case 4. One may lie out of habit without intending to deceive anyone.

Case 5. If a lie must intend to deceive, you could never ask anyone to tell you a lie. If they do try, it would not be a lie because you already know it is an attempt to deceive.

II. A. A New Theory of Lying

We may now give a new definition. It will account for all of the previous examples. A lie is believing (or knowing) one thing and saying (writing, or expressing) another. To lie is like a "speech-mask."[8] You may express a lie merely by a gesture. The liar must be aware that the belief and the statement are different. For example, you say, "London is the capital of West Germany," though you know that it is not. You may, for example, shrug your shoulders as if you do not know, when you do know.

The philosopher Justus Hartnack (1972) supports this definition as follows:

> If I assert that something is the case and my assertion is false, I may be lying—but of course need not be. If I am convinced

> of the truth of my assertion and it nevertheless is false, I am mistaken but am not lying. But if I know or have good reason to believe that my assertion is false, I am lying—and I am lying even if my assertion turns out to be true.

Another philosopher Donald Davidson wrote (1979):

> Telling a lie requires not that what you say be false but that you think it false . . . (p. 41).

Kant wrote (1930):

> Not every untruth is a lie; it is a lie only if I have expressly given the other to understand that I am willing to acquaint him with my thought. (p. 228)

Dictionaries often give several contradictory definitions. This is also true of **Webster's** (1981). A definition of lying which contradicts the others is that a lie is:

> An assertion of something known or believed to be untrue; a deliberate misrepresenting of fact with intent to deceive.

The first part agrees with our new definition. The second part is unacceptable and has been refuted.

In support of the new view, we may quote Wittgenstein:

> Lying about what I see . . . is knowing

> what I see and saying something else. (1968, p. 280)

B. Nineteen Characteristics of Lying.

On this new definition:[9]

1. A lie is not the same as making a false statement.[10]

2. A lie is not the same as not telling the objective truth.

3. If we say what we believe, it is not a lie, but it may be a false statement. We may say, "He doesn't lie, he just does not know the truth."

4. A statement itself cannot be a lie. It is a relationship between two statements. It must be compared to one's belief in order to see if it is a lie. A lie, therefore, is not a thing, an untruth.[11]

5. A liar may by mistake say something which is true while believing that it is false.

6. You can lie and at the same time tell what other people think is a truth. This is when you do not think it is true.[12]

7. A lie is merely a contradiction between belief (self-talk) and expression. In itself it is not good or bad. It is neutral as such.[13]

Jeremy Bentham said the same thing in slightly more complex language:[3]

> Falsehood, take it by itself, consider it as not being accompanied by any other

> material circumstances, nor therefore productive of any material effects, can never upon the principle of utility, constitute any offense at all.

8. A lie is like the wind: pleasant, cool breezes in summer to help sustain life, but threatening and dangerous in winter. In itself, the wind is neither good nor bad. A lie is a lie, whether or not one wishes to do harm by telling it. By lying, the consequences may be good or bad or both. Sometimes we may produce the greatest good for the greatest number of people by lying. For example, tell a harmless lie to save an innocent person's life. It is a lie no matter whether the consequences are harmful or helpful. A lie is not bad in itself. It depends on what we do with it. Kant (1930) wrote:

> A lie is a lie . . . whether it be told with good or bad intent . . . But if a lie does no harm to anyone and no one's interests are affected by it, is it a lie? Certainly. (p. 228)

Contradiction and false definitions may be more harmful than lies. A lie may be considered to be only one type of logical fallacy. It deviates from adequate argument.

9. A lie is a lie whether or not one wishes it to be believed. It is a lie whether or not it is believed. You can lie to your car, though it will not understand you.

10. Similarly, a true statement is true whether or not it has harmful consequences. Some people would be hurt by knowing certain truths. You may not want to know exactly what your enemies think of you.

11. Lying is subjective in that it depends only on what one happens to believe, rather than on objective truth. The truth differs for different people and different societies. Someone else's falsity may be your truth.

12. We cannot lie about things we do not know or have beliefs about. One exception to this is that we may say we know when we do not. But even to believe (or know) we do not believe (know) is still to believe (know). Also it is a lie to say we believe when we know, or that we know when we merely believe.

13. We may lie about the strength or extent of our belief. It is a lie to say we know a foreign language when we know we know only a few words.

14. Words are often abstract or unclear and so can hide what one really believes. We can lie by using unclear language. There are, then, many degrees of lying. Vague or general language can even be a clue to lying. The dictionary calls this type of lying, "prevarication." "Prevarication" comes from words meaning "walk crookedly." It thus means to deviate from the subjective truth.

15. We may contradict ourselves without

lying. Our belief may just have changed. One may contradict oneself because of confusion about one's beliefs, and so not be lying. More will be said about this under the topic of "self-lie," "life-lie," and "liar paradox."

16. An insane person who utters clearly impossible or false statements, but believes them, is not lying. For example, to say "I am a rabbit," may not be a lie to an insane person. Therapists are often not clear about this.

17. To lie, the liar must *be aware* that what is stated is different than the belief.

18. It is not a lie if you try, but still cannot say what you mean.

19. If a lie is not in itself harmful, we need not be blamed merely for lying. It is the consequence which is good or bad. We may be praised for a life-saving lie and blamed for a harmful lie. Sidgwick wrote, "There seems to be circumstances under which the code of honor [requires] lying."[3]

C. Chart Comparing the Old and New View of Lying

A chart may be useful to contrast the old and new definitions. Let "T" be a true statement and "F" be a false statement. But do not think that all statements must be completely true or false. And note that true and false are often vague terms used out of context. So our chart is only a model or fiction which may be useful to give some insight. A statement may be true for one person, but objectively false. We have these possibilities:

	Column I	Column II	Column III
Row	Person Believes	Person Says	Objective Belief or What People Believe
1	T	T	T
2	T	T	F
3	T	F	T
4	T	F	F
5	F	T	T
6	F	T	F
7	F	F	T
8	F	F	F

On the new definition that a lie is knowingly saying (Column II) other than what one believes (Column I), the following are lies: Rows 3, 4, 5, 6.

On the old definition that a lie is telling (Column II) an objective untruth (Column III), the following are lies: Rows 2, 3, 6, 7. The failure of the old definition is that in rows 2 and 7, the person is in fact not lying, but is said to lie. (Here you are said to be lying merely because you disagree with others. They, however, may falsely think you are really lying.) In rows 4 and 5 the person actually is lying, but is seen not to be lying. This is often referred to as "telling people what they want to believe." In this way, it is the big lies which may go unnoticed in a society.

In rows 3 and 6, you agree with the common view of truth, and so on both definitions it is a lie. In general, on the old definition, if you disagree with people you are said to lie. Some see as a lie whatever disagrees with one's own personal views.

III. A. Self-Lie[14]

"The most common lie is the lie one tells to oneself." Nietzsche[37]

"The final belief is to believe in a fiction, which you know to be a fiction." Wallace Stevens

Self-lie refers to our lying to ourselves. That is easy to say. But what does it mean? How can we lie to our own selves?[15] At first glance, it seems like a contradiction out of **Alice in Wonderland:**

"I can't believe that!" said Alice.
"Can't you?" the Queen said in a pitying tone. "Try again: draw a long breath, and shut your eyes."
Alice laughed. "There's no use trying," she said: "one can't believe impossible things."

How do we come to believe what we do not believe? How could we? How dare we? By just taking a long breath, and shutting our eyes, as the Queen suggests?

To make the paradox more clear it would seem that lying to ourselves is something like the following:

a. loving your enemy.

b. believing that black is white.

c. believing that you can take a bath without getting wet.

d. seeing a smile without a face.

e. gossiping about yourself "behind your back."

f. keeping secrets from yourself.

g. accusing yourself of something you know you did not do.

h. believing that you are your sister.

i. asking yourself if you are asleep.

j. remembering the future.

k. hiding your true feelings from yourself.

l. cheating yourself.

m. giving yourself very good advice, but very seldom following it.

To lie to yourself is supposedly to believe what you do not believe. You believe it is raining when you know that it is not raining. But you cannot believe what you do not believe. This is one paradox of the self-lie.[16] (See also Martin 1985)

The poetess Emily Dickinson wrote:

> Believing what we don't believe does not exhilarate.

John Dewey wrote:

> Acknowledgment that we do not know what we do not know is a necessity of all intellectual integrity. (1934)

How, then, can we lie to ourselves if it is a contradiction to do so? On the new definition the solution is easy. We merely tell ourselves other than what we believe. We say it, but do not believe it. It is a kind of self-talk or self-command. Thus, we are not required to believe what we do not believe. John is short. He says to himself, "John you are a giraffe. You have got height. Consider going into basketball." He does not believe he is tall, he just says he is. There is, then, no contradiction.

Self-lie is seen now as the relation of only what (a) a person believes, and (b) says. It has nothing to do with objective truth or what other people think (unless we take on other's views as our own). In the following chart, let "T" be a true statement and "F" be a false statement. The possibilities of self-lie are roughly as follows:

	Column I	Column II
Row	Person Believes	Person Says
1	T	T
2	T	F
3	F	T
4	F	F

Only rows 2 and 3 are lies. On the new view, even lies to others would also be self-lies. If you say something is false, but are not aware that you think that it is true, you are not lying. You are mistaken. To lie, you must knowingly intend to express to yourself other than what you believe.

Self-lie, then, seems to be pointless. What reason is there to tell ourselves what we do not believe? We believe a person is tall but we say to ourselves that she is short. It is irrational to say that. It is like saying, "I disagree very strongly with myself."

Some attempts to make sense of why we would lie to ourselves are:

a. We are really somehow two or more selves, a divided self, and to lie to ourselves is like one person lying to another. But this equivocates with self and is not a self-lie.

b. We tell ourselves other than what we only *partially* believe. This equivocates with "belief."

c. We are not really conscious that we contradict ourselves. Then it is not a self-lie. A similar case is when we are not clear what we believe, and without thinking we say we believe a number of things.

d. We say one thing but, without noticing it, do another. This is not a self-lie. If we consciously do another, this is a self-lie. It is a conscious expression of other than what we believe.

e. Most people do consciously hold two or more contradictory beliefs. It can be pointed out to them they are clearly contradictory. Yet we still hold those beliefs. But this, too, is not a self-lie because both statements *are* believed. A self-lie is expressing to oneself *other* than what is believed. One of the best examples is believing that (1) we will only believe something if we have good evidence, and also (2) believing in the supernatural. We may have no evidence that time or force exist as entities, yet believe that they do.

f. We consciously believe what we do not believe. This is a paradox. Either it does not make sense, or we are using "believe" in different senses, that is, we are equivocating.

Thus, we can lie to ourselves, but it seems pointless to do so. And we are conscious of the lie, so we are not deceiving ourselves.

One main purpose of lying is to change the beliefs of others. So one may lie to oneself to change one's own beliefs in the future. We can do this by (a) education, (b) indoctrination, or (c) by faulty thinking. To do it by education is like overcoming prejudices. Here you lie to yourself because you wish to replace your false belief with a true belief.

You wish to overcome your false belief. In this sense, education is a form of lying! It replaces false ideas with true ones.

If you try to deny a true idea by censorship, indoctrination, or faulty thinking, it is the reverse of education. But it is still a self-lie. In sum, we may lie to ourselves not to believe now what we do not believe now, but in order to change our beliefs. We may call this "self-caused-deception." As "fraud" refers to intentional deception resulting in injury, we may also call it "defrauding oneself."

We may change our beliefs critically or uncritically. Education promotes critical change. Fallacious thinking promotes irrational change. This is why we might be interested in the idea of self-lie. We want to say that a self-lie is unacceptable if it is based on irrational thinking. The question of self-lies which deceive is also the question, "How can one be consciously or unconsciously irrational?" How could one learn to believe that what is false is true?

Some synonyms of self-deception are: insincerity, self-persuasion, self-hypnosis; logical fallacies such as contradiction, circularity, assuming what you wish to prove, etc.; hypocrisy, forgetting, double-morality, indoctrination, repetition, censorship; defense-mechanisms such as sublimation, repression and rationalization, etc.

These are the sorts of irrational methods by which we can deceive ourselves. There comes a point at which we have to lose consciousness of our being deceived.

In short, self-deception is faulty thinking. It is a "scandal of belief," not a self-lie, but self-lie may be used to try to deceive ourselves in the future. Education based on mere memorization, repetition and lack of critical thinking is an example of a self-lie. Some deliberately choose not to be critical. Thinking is not important to them. They do not want to know, and strive against true understanding. They are anti-inquiry. It is self-imposed ignorance.[17] The lie injures oneself.[18]

This tendency to lie to ourselves is expressed by the following statements:

"I will not change my mind no matter what you say."

"I'll never believe that."

"I refuse to discuss it."

"I don't need evidence, I just know it's true."

"Most people believe it, so it must be true."

"I have a special intuition."

"Some things are true without proof."

"I say I will do it, but I know I won't."

"I accept all the arguments against it, but I still think it is true."

"Why bother to inquire, I know all I need to know."

"I will believe what I want to believe."

The philosopher Paul Kurtz (1977) wrote:

> All too often human beings are eager to abandon the use of their reason. (p. 54)

Nietzsche said:

> Not to question, not to tremble with the craving and the joy of questioning . . . that is what I find to be *contemptible* . . . (**The Gay Science** Book I, #2).
>
> By lie I mean: wishing *not* to see something that one does see.[37]

Basically, self-deception is accomplished by suppression of reason, or following the less reasonable argument.

Fingarette (1969) holds a similar view:

> The self-deceiver is one whose life-situation is such that, on the basis of his tacit assessment of his situation, he finds there is overriding reason for adopting a policy of not spelling out some engagement of his in the world. (p. 62) (See also Mele.)

The self-deceiver may just be unskilled with language. We use over-abstract terms or do not realize we contradict ourselves. It is not a self-lie, but it is self-deception. It is also clumsy thinking.

Fingarette mentioned the importance of language skills in lying. (p. 51) He wrote:

> He means to tell both us and himself the way things are, but he is unskilled in expressing matters. (p. 53)

Plack (1976) states that the main medium of lying and self-deception is language.[19] To avoid self-deception we must increase our knowledge and especially our skills with language use. Wittgenstein (1958) stated,

> Lying is a language-game that needs to be learned like any other. (#249)[1]

Thinking is basically a use of language. The lie is a rhetorical device like irony or metaphor. To clarify our language is to clarify our thinking. To understand lying is to understand the language of lying, its uses and misuses. It is often said that all thinking is metaphorical. To clarify our thinking we must clarify our metaphors.

An important distinction must be made between (a) lying to oneself, and (b) others saying we are lying to ourselves. If we are not aware that we are lying to ourselves, it is not a lie, even if others say so. If others say we are lying to ourselves they must have evidence that we are saying other than what we believe. They are often not in a good position to know that. But what they can know is that we are objectively deceiving ourselves. While we are deceived we usually cannot know that. One important use, then, of self-lie is when it refers to other people to indicate that they are deceiving themselves. It may not be literally true that one is lying to oneself, but there may be self-deception. "He is lying to himself" may only mean, "He is deceiving himself." It exposes and brings attention to one's contradictory behavior.

Nietzsche saw that it is easy to criticize other's beliefs, but that the most difficult thing is to criticize one's own. He wrote:

> I am that which must always overcome itself. The worst enemy you can encounter will always be you, yourself; you lie in wait for yourself in caves and woods. (**Thus Spoke Zarathustra**)[37]

We have learned to protect ourselves from some of the lies others tell us, but less often from the careless thinking or the lies we tell ourselves. It is one use of the idea of self-lie to call attention to that to encourage us to question our thoughts and feelings to make sure they are genuine. One synonym of self-lie is insincerity. To protect ourselves against false beliefs and negative emotions is to protect ourselves against the self-lie and self-deception. It is to be our best self.

B. Life-Lie[20]

If anything may be said to be of lasting value from the philosopher Socrates, it is the asking of questions. The resistance to being asked questions is probably as great today as it was then. People do not want to inquire "too much," question "too much." It is thought to be anti-social. This refusal to inquire is a form of life-lie which Socrates exposed. He showed that people claim to know, but when questioned, do not know. Socrates himself avoided this self-lie by claiming that he did not claim to know. He professed ignorance.

The Socratic method supposedly only "drew out" knowledge which was in others. Socrates asked questions he supposedly did not know the answers to in advance. The person questioned was found not to know the answers either. This made Socrates look either brilliant in his ignorance, or a nuisance, a meddler. Those who claimed to know were seen to be committing what we may call a life-lie. But Socrates himself knew in advance that those questioned would not know the answers, so he too committed a life-lie.

Another sense of Socratic method is to ask questions he already himself knows the answer to. This sort of question can trap those questioned. In this case, Socrates pretended not to know the answers he in fact knew. Again, a life-lie.

The kinds of questions Socrates asked were of the form, "What is the definition of X?" For example, "What is the definition of Justice?" The politician answered, "Justice is doing what agrees with the laws." Then, Socrates would point out that the definition is inadequate because we often change the laws because they are unfair. And, furthermore, for whatever definition was given, Socrates would find an exception. Again, this would make Socrates look brilliant, or at least a troublesome person. Few people are thankful for losing their cherished beliefs. Henrik Ibsen wrote in **The Wild Duck**, "Take away the life-lie from the average person, and you take his happiness along with it."[21] Socrates could easily make himself an "enemy of the people."

We may now also take away some of Socrates' happiness. He assumed that "Justice," "Truth," "Good," "Time," and other words do in fact have single absolute definitions. But if no absolute definitions are to be found, Socrates was asking for the impossible. He was asking the impossible not only of others, but of himself. He was tricked by his own question. He was looking for something he could never find. An answer to the question, "What is the definition of X?" is that it is a faulty question. It is in this way also that Socrates held a life-lie. He spent his life asking questions which do not have answers. With a life-lie we work ourselves into such a position that we are trapped. We trap ourselves.

Without looking for the definition of life-lie we can nevertheless suggest different examples and types.[22]

A life-lie is expressing other than what is believed about one's life. It may be:

1. a disagreement between expressed behavior and one's own "conscience" (that is, self-talk).

2. believing you are what you are not (e.g., superiority or inferiority complexes).

3. self-lie (or self-deception) to try to protect ourselves from ideas which we think will harm us.

4. failure to agree with arguments even when we know they are correct. Failure to change a view in light of new evidence.

5. denial of truth.

6. being less than coherent.

7. conflicts between thought and experience.

8. conflicts between thought and thought (or between statements held as true).[23]

Life-lie may be used metaphorically to mean self-deception. What you believe about your life may be objectively false. Life-lie may include other kinds of lies.[24] It may be said to oneself as well as to others. And it may involve faulty philosophies or philosophies of life.[25]

Some examples of life-lie are:

1. pretending to be happy when you are not.

2. pretending to believe in something without evidence. This is bias or prejudice. The philosopher John Wilson (1960) wrote:

> The worst possible thing is to imagine that we know when we do not know: it is far better to confess ignorance than to pretend to false knowledge. (p. 74)

3. the belief that you must be liked by everyone.

4. the belief that you or life can always be perfect.

5. following authority and society blindly.

6. believing that people can be just bad in themselves.

7. the belief that punishment is the best way to cure criminal behavior.

8. the belief that "blood is thicker than water," and accordingly family members will always be kind to you.

9. bragging, hypocrisy; and so on.

Life-lies often involve faulty questions and/or faulty answers. "What am I really?", or "Who am I really?" are such faulty questions. They are vague, obscure questions and it is not clear what the answer would ever be. Consider the question, "What is life all about?" The answer could be, "Deceiving ourselves."

We cannot answer, "Who are you really?" You are a student. You are young. You are a person. But you are no one thing such that we can say that that is what you really are. "You" has no single definition. This is the "problem of the self."

We create ourselves by the way we see ourselves. If we see ourselves in faulty ways, it is a life-lie. But it is a life-lie to think there is only one real "me." We need not try to find out who we "really" are. "Really" doesn't make sense here. Again, we may quote Ibsen (**Peer Gynt**):

> One question only, what is it, 'to be yourself,' in truth? (Scene 5)

Life-lie has also been seen as our playing a role in society and then erroneously thinking that the role is the real thing. "He no longer distinguishes his nature from the role which he plays, he deceives himself."[26]

The Madam Bovary complex involves completely, or largely, assuming the personality of another person (Eck, 1970, pp. 112ff.). We may conceal ourselves behind titles, social class, professions, or snobbery. We may hide behind what a society erroneously thinks is acceptable, such as war. Philosophers and humanists often maintain that metaphysics and any belief in the supernatural is a form of life-lie.

Several other life-lie questions are:

a. What is the real meaning of life?

b. What is really the only truth?

c. What was I really meant to do?

d. What really is my true identity?

e. What is a woman or man really?

We create theories and models about our political, religious, social, scientific, psychological, philosophical, intellectual and emotional lives. These are just useful fictions or models. They change with new evidence and knowledge. If we take such models or metaphors literally, we create illusions. This is to commit the "metaphor-to-myth" fallacy. That is, to take only one theory or metaphor as being the only way to interpret something is to create a myth or false view. It is like saying, "I am just a student, nothing else." This is only one metaphor.

A life-lie, generally speaking, is expressing other than what we believe. So if we hold a false belief it is not a lie. On the other hand, by education we may see it to be false and so a lie. That is, we may change our beliefs. We may study to be a teacher, but find we prefer medical work. We had chosen the wrong profession. We may think we are producing the greatest good for the most people, only to realize that we buy trivial things while people are starving. As in this case, the many contradictions in lives can create life-lies.

We create roles for ourselves and we play those roles. We create the life we live. We live our metaphors or "lies." If we are aware that they are just roles or fictions, they are not lies. We can even say, "Now, I will choose 'lies' for my life." Try to choose the best ones available. We live our metaphors.

IV. Thought and Language: Rejection of Mentalism and Abstraction

A. Mentalism

The language and style used so far is ordinary—all too ordinary. In terms of recent research some of it is not acceptable. We can no longer use language as we used to, in the ordinary way. We must now criticize our own theory. We will not reject it, but qualify it. We must further define our terms.

Lying was defined on the new theory as: conscious expression of other than what we believe. The same theory may be expressed by substituting synonyms as follows:

conscious

knowing
intentional
deliberate
aware

expression

saying
affirming
writing
maintaining
stating
meaning
convincing
(body-language or
gesturing)
behaving
expressing of ideas

of other than

the opposite of
more than
less than
something different than

what we

I
self
mind

believe.

think
intend
know
say to myself
understand
experience
feel
wish

For example, the definition above may be rephrased as: deliberate writing of something different than what I say to myself. Many alternate formulations may accordingly be given. If we are to define our terms we must define also all of the different synonyms.

For the average person, there is no problem with words such as mind, meaning, knowing, conscious, etc. For many philosophers, psychologists and linguists, to speak of such "things" without clarification would be outrageous. For example, we cannot just speak of "meaning" without giving evidence that there is such a thing. Perhaps the one thing that characterizes twentieth century critical thinking more than any other, is the critique of language. We can no longer merely speak or write as we used to. We must now carefully examine our language first. In doing this we upset many of our previous views.

This has, for example, been referred to as "The Revolution in Philosophy." (Ayer 1965) It also applies to most other subjects of study.

For each word used above we must ask, What does it mean? What is it like? What evidence do we have for it? What purpose does it serve? When this is done the above terms can be classified in terms of certain areas of inquiry such as the problem of the self, problem of whether or not there are inner, private states, problems of meaning, etc. Some quotations will be given to show that many of the above terms are to be rejected in their usual uses.

Problem of the Self: What do we mean by I, me, the self, you, etc.? Am I a mind and body? Is the normal and insane self to be treated the same in, "He is lying"? In "I lie to myself," is the "I" the mind? Does the mind lie to itself? Descartes, of course, is especially known for his analysis of the self as mind and body, and most still believe that. This view is in radical contrast to the following:

> Constructions such as mind-body . . . have brought much mythology into the study of *Homo sapiens*. . . . Consider the utter vacuity of such expressions as 'man is mind,' . . . (Observer 1978)

> Mind is a ghost in the machine. . . . The phrase 'in the mind' can and should always be dispensed with. (Ryle 1949)

> Semantic theory should avoid commitment with respect to the philosophical and psychological status of 'concepts,' 'ideas' and the 'mind.' (p. 474) Many philosophers and psychologists are extremely dubious about the existence of 'concepts,' or indeed of the 'mind.' (John Lyons 1968)

> The mind is not a thing, or a substance, distinct from the body. (Cornforth 1963, p. 11)

Mind is a pseudo-psychological fiction. The literature shows that we have no clear definition of it, no empirical evidence for it. "Do I have a mind?" is not an intelligible or genuine question, and so can have no answer. We may drop "mind" from our vocabulary as being a myth. We nevertheless even find many, if not most, academic writers continuing to speak of mind. It is ironic that one writer recently used the word "mind" incorrectly ten times in two pages in a book attempting to clarify irrationality. (Pears 1984, pp. 6-7) We must have a better analysis of the self. If we say "I lie," what do we mean by "I"? How does "I" enter into lying?

Again on the usual view, what we mean is that "I" refers to thinking, knowing, believing, intending, feeling, etc. These are usually called "mental processes," "private states," or "internal states." They are supposedly states or things like ideas or emotions going on within us. But, once more, contemporary research does not let us use such terms without objection:

> Mental processes are just queer. (Wittgenstein 1958, #363)
>
> We talk of processes and states and leave their nature undecided. . . . So we have to deny the yet uncomprehended process in the yet unexplored medium. (Wittgenstein 1958, #308)
>
> Thought is simply *behavior* — verbal or nonverbal, covert or overt. It is not some mysterious process responsible for behavior but the very behavior itself in all the complexity of its controlling relations . . . (Skinner 1957, p. 449)
>
> We repudiate mental entities as entities. . . .It is moot indeed whether the positing of additional objects of a mental kind is a help or a hindrance to science. (Quine 1966, pp. 213-214)

Hundreds of similar quotations could be cited. It is now clear that we cannot just assume the existence of ideas, thoughts, beliefs, knowledge, etc. In fact, we do not have evidence for them as such. We never see, feel, or "catch" an idea. Like "mind," to think there are "ideas" as such, is a myth. We do not have evidence for them. They can no longer be thought of as invisible atoms which combine to create a kind of "mental chemistry." So we cannot use such mentalistic terms to describe lying.

We cannot say lying is literally "thinking" one thing, but saying another. We cannot simply say lying is saying other than what we "believe." We must first find out what is meant by belief. Belief is not just a private, internal, mental state. The same clarification is needed for all of the mentalistic words used as synonyms earlier such as: knowing, intending, awareness, conscious, understanding, feeling, etc. Most writers still ignore these criticisms, but they cannot be ignored without doing serious injustice to inquiry. To ignore them would be a form of self-lie or self-deception.

B. Meaning

We have now presented two forms of mentalism: (1) "mind" as a myth, and (2) "mental processes" such as internal "ideas" for which we fail to have evidence. We may also add (3) meaning. "Meaning" is a synonym of "idea," so if we lack evidence for ideas we lack evidence for meaning. That is, on the common definition of "meaning," a word stands for an idea or concept. We cannot assume that we just have non-linguistic ideas and then put them into words. If there are no ideas, there are no meanings. Once again, contemporary literature (and often ancient literature) crisply opposes the common view. The following are typical expressions of the view that "meaning" may be seen as a myth:

> Ghostly entities such as meanings, sense, or ideas provide no more than the ghost of an explanation. (I. Scheffler 1979)

> An adequate science of meaning must dispense with mentalistic psychology along with its notion of meaning as the psychic counterpart of word-things of every type. . . . We have referred to the futility and inutility of the prevailing mentalistic postulation of the majority of students of language meaning . . . (**Observer** 1976, pp. 442,444)

> Characterizing meaning merely in terms of concepts is unexplanatory. (Kempson 1977, p. 17)

> The notion of there being a fixed, explicable, and as yet unexplained meaning in the speaker's mind is gratuitous. (Quine 1964)

Mythical meaning has appeared in more recent literature as a "speech act." (Searle 1969) A mental "act" can be just as mentalistic as meaning. (Kempson 1977)

We cannot, then, define lying as "Having one meaning, but expressing another." This will not work unless we are clear about what meaning is. We may instead say, "I have said X, but intended to say Y."

C. Thought as Language

Now mentalism in all of its forms has been rejected. A new non-mentalistic theory of belief, thinking and meaning, etc. must be developed (Shibles 1972). The way in which this has been done is to reduce thinking and meaning to language. By thought we basically mean language. Several statements of this view are:

> The old empiricist looked inward upon his ideas; the new empiricist looks outward upon the social institution of language. (Quine 1969)

> When I think in language, there aren't 'meanings' going through my mind in addition to the verbal expressions: The language is itself the vehicle of thought. (#329)
> Is thinking a kind of speaking? (#330) (Wittgenstein 1958)

> Language cannot be considered as a simple instrument . . . of thought. (Barthes 1972, p. 156)

> Thought is realized and can be realized in language only. (Max Müller 1887)

> There is no thinking, there is only speaking. Thinking is speaking . . . (Mauthner. See Weiler 1970)

> I believe that the identification of knowing and thinking with speech is wholly in the right direction. (John Dewey 1922, p. 561)

To think is like self-talk. This view is held by a number of contemporary therapists. (A. Ellis 1962, 1977)

The list of those who, to some or a large extent, reduce thought to language would be long. We do not have two things: thought and language, but one: language. In opposition to the common view, we do not "express" or "press out" our ideas into words. We do not pour ideas into words as we pour milk into glasses. We have no "ideas" as such, only words.

And language is something we have evidence for. It is not claimed that this is a complete view or an absolutely true view. It is, however, an extremely useful model. The full arguments for replacing thought with language would require an analysis of most of the contemporary and some of the traditional schools of thought.

The mentalistic terms used earlier to define lying, may now be reduced to language models. Thinking, knowing, believing are certain language-games. A detailed way in which mental terms may be reduced to nonmental ones is given in **Wittgenstein, Language and Philosophy** (Shibles 1969). There the term "intention" is analyzed. It will also help us to understand what is meant by such statements as, "Lying is intentionally saying other than what we believe."

However, an analysis of "I believe," and "I know," would involve the entire discipline of epistemology. For our present argument I wish only to point out that any such theories should be nonmentalistic and should stress actual language. It is partly for this reason that the new theory of lying is called "new." This theory has not appeared in the tradition in this form. (See Weinrich 1966)

It should be mentioned that not all kinds of sayings and statements can be lies. Could the following be lies?

(a) "What time is it?" Can questions be lies?

(b) "Hello."

(c) "Ouch."

(d) "Please pass the sugar."

Such statements seem not capable of being lies. There may be lies associated with them. We can say, "I said, 'Hello' but I didn't mean it." Or you want to ask for money, but instead ask, "What time is it?" By examining our language in this way we may find out about the rich subtlety of lying. It is also a qualification of the definition that lying is saying to others other than what we are saying to ourselves. When someone says, "Please pass the sugar," we would not ordinarily say that it is a lie. On the theory the following question arises. If one says:

(a) "Please pass the sugar,"

but thinks

(b) "You had better pass the sugar or else,"

is it a lie? It is.

We can even lie with expletives, or intensifiers such as: Well!, Really?, indeed, too, so, merely, simply, just, anyway. For example, say just before leaving:

"Well, I guess it is about time to go."

How is "well" used here? How are we to take it? Whatever its use, it can have a misuse. We can lie about it. We can lie when we say, "Come on, then!" Linguists, and logicians especially, have largely neglected the study of such words. Therefore, how we lie with them is also in need of research. Meanwhile, when someone says, "Hello," we can wonder if they are lying. To not grasp this point is to fail to understand the theory of lying and the subtlety of language.

D. Abstraction

It would be difficult to explain to most people what abstraction is or that there is a problem with it. Here abstract terms are those which seem to refer to something. But on inquiry nothing can be found. Mentalism produced a number of examples, but there are others. "Truth," for example, seems to refer to something. However, in a later section it will be seen that there is no truth in itself. "Do you swear to tell the whole Truth?" is a misuse of language.

The fallacy of abstractionism is uncritical use of vague terms, e.g., cause, energy, idea, number, mind, force, soul, space, time. General terms can be reduced to specific instances, abstract terms as such, cannot. As can be seen, many familiar, everyday terms are on this list. They are so common that it is hard for people to believe that there could be something wrong with them. What is not ordinarily controversial, such as time, is in the literature immensely controversial.

Abstract terms are identified by lack of intelligibility, lack of evidence, or by the inability to give examples of what is meant. Other examples of abstract terms are love, emotion, reason, infinity, being, person, good, bad, etc.

A synonym of abstraction is essentialism. It is thought that because nothing concrete can be found for a word to refer to, it must refer to an "essence." This is fairly much what Plato believed (called "Platonism"). But "essence" derives from *esse* meaning "to be." An essence means only that something exists. To say a word refers to an essence is to say nothing at all. It is not evidence.

And Plato does an excellent job of refuting his own theory in his dialogue, **Parmenides.**

Another synonym is "symbol." But symbol is not evidence either. The word "truth" cannot symbolize "Truth." Truth is not a thing as a book is a thing. Abstraction is also indicated by the phrase "in itself," and by the word "absolute" as in:

Duty in itself.
Truth in itself.
Time itself.
The absolute Truth.
The absolute Good.

The above commit the fallacy of abstractionism. Another example is given in the following:

> 'Emotions,' 'cognitions,' and 'mind' are not connected with behavior of organisms but with abstractions and nonexistent psychic entities. . . . Verbal abstractions are made into timeless and spaceless things like Platonic ideas eternally existing in a world beyond the heavens. (**Observer** 1981, pp. 599, 603)

The following are some abstract terms related especially to lying: lie, truth, belief, objective or absolute truth, the self, our understanding, consciousness, promise. We tend to think these terms refer to things. A lie is not a thing. It is not even something that can be told. We personify it as if it were a human. A lie is rather a relationship between statements. We can tell or utter a statement, but not literally tell a lie. "To tell a lie" is a metaphorical way of speaking.

We speak about lies as if they could be wrapped in packages, displaced in water or sold. Beliefs are not things or entities either. It is misleading then to say that a lie is to say other than what we believe. What is a belief here? It is not a thought. It could be self-talk, one or a group of related statements. A belief need not be one thing or one statement. And although self-talk and imagery cannot be regarded as an internal state, we have evidence for them.

We say we have degrees of belief or knowledge as we have degrees of temperature. Degrees do not directly apply here. Beliefs refer to statements and the way in which they relate to or cohere with one another. Does "You believe X," mean you would stake your life on it? Belief may mean we take a statement as true without evidence. It is to comment on a statement, for a certain purpose only, to say that it is true or false. Neither do beliefs change. We instead change our statements. Just as the "Self" is not an entity in itself, "Belief" is not an entity in itself.

The erroneous use in this way of abstract terms may also be called "rationalism." A recent typical example of this misuse is:

> . . . The true agent is his reason, the authority within him. . . . It is so obvious that reason ought to control the guest's appetite . . . . Ask him to control his rational desire . . . . Reason happens to be our most reliable guide to action. This is because reason is much more adaptable than its rivals, emotion and appetite. (p. 17) Irrationality is incorrect processing of information in the mind. (p. 14) (Pears 1984)

To be intelligible, abstract terms must be reduced to concrete statements used in concrete cases of language usage. With this qualification I may now qualify my own statements in this book. They are only intelligible if they can be reduced to such cases. This is sometimes referred to as the "case method" of doing philosophy. We can see how simplistic and unacceptable it is to say, "A lie is telling an untruth."

"A lie is really . . ." This is also absolutism. The new definition given in this book is intended not as an absolute definition. It is only a descriptive model of looking at lying in order to better understand it and in order to prevent abuse. It is a descriptive, pragmatic definition. That it contains elements of stipulation and ethical or persuasive definition is not denied. But the main point is that the model is not seen to be absolutely true or absolutely complete or the only way of analyzing lying. Thus, the theory does not commit the metaphor-to-myth fallacy of taking one's theory literally.

Another form is ethical absolutism such as, "Lies are wrong in themselves." An example of this form is: "The noblest purpose will not justify a lie."[27] Kant also held an absolutist view, as was discussed earlier.[28]

Fichte holds the absolutist view:

What results from the lie is never good.[29]

V. More Complex Words Which Suggest Lying[30]

a. Hypocrisy. For example, you say you will not do a certain thing, but find you end up doing it. You tell yourself you will not believe anything without evidence, but do believe things without evidence. One reason lying is thought bad is that it is, like hypocrisy, pretending to be what you are not.

b. Dogma. (Fixed belief without evidence.) If we believe in dogma we are lying to ourselves or deceiving ourselves.

c. Insincerity. When we write without expressing what we feel and believe or want, we are not being honest with ourselves or others. (Winston Churchill, the former British Prime Minister, called this kind of lying "Terminological inexactitude," that is, incorrect words.) Good writing style often involves sincerity, being genuine or honest. The philosopher John Wilson wrote (1963):

> Perhaps the most important quality which you should seek after in writing . . . is the quality of honesty. (p. 46)

d. Euphemism. We replace an unpleasant word with a word which sounds better. Instead of, "death," we say, "passed away." "Cemetery" comes from a word meaning, "sleeping place." We say the animal doctor "put the cat to sleep," instead of, "He killed the cat." If we begin to believe the euphemism is true we lie to ourselves.

Euphemisms are also used to lie to others. "Buy this land. Plenty of fresh air and water available." We may find we bought a swamp.

The poet Robert Browning wrote:

> 'Lied' is a rough phrase; say he fell from the truth.

Some legal terms for lying to others are the following:

e. Libel. A false and harmful written statement about someone. This may not be a lie if the person believes the false statement to be true. The law may still charge a person with libel if the statement harms one's reputation. This may involve a cartoon which is a false picture of a person and makes one look silly or look like a criminal.

f. Slander. Saying false and harmful things about someone. The false statement may accuse one of a crime or immoral act. It may be name-calling, ridicule, insults. It is like libel except that it is spoken rather than written.

Libel and slander may be illegal even if they are given in jest, or ironically, even if hinted at. It is often illegal even to joke about someone carrying a bomb on an airplane.

g. Perjury. This is a legal term also. In United States law it is lying about the facts of a crime while under oath. The oath is swearing to tell the truth, in the courtroom. To be a lie, perjury must be a false statement (or sometimes true) and be made knowingly. If a statement is false, but the witness believes it is true, it is not a lie. Thus, the test of perjury agrees with our definition of lying as saying what one does not believe.

On the other hand, on a second, contradictory view of perjury, the court may assume that you are lying if you contradict yourself or say inconsistent things even if you say what you believe. We do sometimes honestly change our beliefs. And we may unknowingly hold contradictory beliefs.

In one case, a man received $1,500 for the sale of land. But under oath he later said that he received only $500. The law often assumes that he lied. But the law may be wrong here if in fact he forgot the correct amount. He may really have believed that he only received $500. The truth or falsity of a statement does not prove it is a lie.

On the other hand, to prove perjury the court must prove that the witness knowingly said what she or he believed to be false. The proof must be given beyond a reasonable doubt. The lie must have been intended rather than made through error, mistake, or due to lack of attention. And it is not perjury if you lie about something not relevant to the case.

Two interesting points made about perjury are that it is lying even if the person (a) tells what is true, but believes it to be false, (b) says something is true when she or he does not know it is true.

In summary, one legal concept of perjury is similar to our definition of lying. Perjury and lying are when a person says other than what she or he believes.

If it is said that you lied in court (perjury) the law says that you may defend yourself by proving the following. These are the "defenses." You may try to show that:

1. What you said is true. (But remember that you can lie by saying what is true if you believe it is false. In that case it is not a defense.)

2. What you said is true in the context or way in which it was said. It was thought to be a lie only because it was not properly understood in the way in which you meant it.

3. You could not remember well.

4. Your thinking was poor. For example, you were too tired, uneducated, ill, or too nervous to think properly.

5. It is likely because of other evidence, that you really believed what you said. You give additional proof to show that you really believed what you said.

6. You corrected your lie at once. You immediately told what you believed to be the truth. Some courts, however, still treat it as perjury even if you immediately afterwards tell the truth.

7. Your life was threatened or you were otherwise forced to tell a lie in court.

It is not a defense to show that no one believed the lie. It is therefore dangerous to joke or use irony in the courtroom.

The law about perjury is complex, sometimes

contradictory, and changing. One case may not be treated the same as the next.

There are written laws about perjury. But we also have to look at the individual court cases and judgments, that is, "case law." It is like clarifying the concept of lying by looking at individual examples or cases. It is an important method to use for understanding generally.

We may compare this account with German law. There, perjury (German word is *Meineid*) is intentional false swearing before the court. The statement uttered must be determined to be false. Thus, if what is said is true, yet you think it false, it is not a lie.[31] Also, only circumstantial evidence is needed to determine if one intended to lie. Stress, then, is placed on the intentional relationship between the belief and the statement.[32]

A similar concept is "false swearing" *(Falscheid)*. Here, one swears to a false statement, while negligently or unreasonably believing it to be true. This concept does include the relationship between belief and statement. Of special interest is that careless false swearing or perjury is not acceptable. If one could have had the correct information, one is expected to have had it. We are to blame for our ignorance. However, exceptional circumstances can lessen or eliminate punishment.[33]

That we are responsible for having the correct information would apply to the case of self-lie and life-lie. It would require that the individual be engaged in continuing education and inquiry.

Some other types of lying are:

h. To make something appear to be what you believe it is not, is to: feign, fake, pretend, be a fraud or imposter.

Fraud is defined in the law as intentional deception resulting in injury to another.It is not the same as lying because lying requires no intent to deceive. However, both require saying other than what is believed. An honestly believed statement is neither a lie nor fraud. For fraud, the following must be present:

1. The statement must be false.

2. The statement must be relevant and important (that is, "material").

3. The defendant must believe it is false.

4. The defendant must intend to deceive (called "scienter") the plaintiff. One may deceive if the statement is made believing it untrue, or not knowing if it is true or false. "Constructive fraud" does not require actual intent, but is assumed from the circumstances.

5. The plaintiff must rely on the statement as much as a careful, reasonable person would. The victim must be ignorant of the falsity but not be *beguiled,* that is, not be ready to be persuaded by the deceiver.

Both lying and fraud involve asserting a statement even when one has no belief or evidence as to the truth or untruth of that statement. If, for example, we assert a statement about religion or science without evidence or not knowing its truth or falsity, we are lying and it is one element of fraud. Another relevant aspect of fraud is that the defendant is not expected to be gullable and not expected to conceal important information. There is a duty to disclose.

i. Many types of false arguments are lies:

1. For example, you say there are flying saucers, though you know you have no evidence to support your belief.

2. Words often have many meanings. To "equivocate" is to seem to be using one meaning, but in fact use another. "I treat everyone equally," may mean "I am fair to everyone," or "I am cruel to everyone, equally." To lie is to misuse our language.

The philosopher Justus Hartnack (1972) wrote:

To lie is to break the rules contained in the logically prior concept of assertion.

To lie is "contra-diction" or contradiction, or anti-speech. The German word for contradiction is *Widerspruch,* that is, against-speech. It is to misuse one use of speaking. It is a failure of communication.

j. Rumor and hearsay are special cases of lying, because here one does not know whether or not the statements or gossip one spreads are true.

k. "Fib." A lie thought to be unimportant; a "white" lie.

l. "Palter." This is to make an unreliable statement of fact or intention. It may be a false promise.

m. "Mendacious" literally means to *mend* or change the truth, and so to lie. It is as if we were to "mend" the truth of our beliefs.

n. False promises. It is a lie to say you will return a loan when you know you never will. It is not necessarily a lie to "break a promise." At the time you make a promise you may truly believe you will carry it out. Promises are not absolute, because circumstances change. Some promises, if kept, would be harmful rather than helpful. Would one keep an unimportant promise if one's life were at stake?

One may promise to always help a friend, but if the friend moves out of the country we may not be able to help her. We then break our promise.

Promises should be qualified. For example, "I promise to help you as much as I reasonably can," or "under ordinary circumstances." One way never to break a promise is not to make one in the first place. We may promise never to make any promises. But this is self-contradictory.

We sometimes promise to hold a belief for the rest of our lives, but as our knowledge grows we may reject the belief. We may promise something we could never do: "I promise that I will live to the age of 200." We may promise something vague: "I promise to love, honor and obey," when we are not at all clear what these words mean. Thus, we hear that "promises were meant to be broken." However, a believed, reasonable and carefully stated promise may well be kept.

Several other forms of promising may be those of being faithful, loyal, trustworthy and dependable. These often involve promising to do certain things.

o. Psychological or therapy terms in lying.

Lying in "mental" patients[34] is not well understood. But people with severe problems of this sort often lie. Lies may be generally classified as delusions, magical thinking, defense-mechanisms, illogical thinking, loss of memory, hallucinations, paranoia, etc. It is not clear what a patient intends or believes when she or he lies. Our analysis of lying may be found useful in helping to understand lying in "mental" patients as well as with "normal" people.

Psychologists and psychiatrists frequently state that they have done little research on lying. They do, however, speak of the following types of lies. These should not, then, be regarded as strictly scientific or well-researched categories.

1. Antisocial personality or conduct disorder. Persistent lying is one sign or example of such disorders. (DSM III)[35]

2. Confabulation. Giving obviously fake accounts of events. Such patients have, for example, falsely stated, "I am in Finland," "I am in a navy kitchen," "I have just delivered a paper on diseases," "Your house is being ripped out of the ground by a giant crane," and so on.[36]

The complete description is not known, so it is not even clear that these are lies. Researchers give conflicting descriptions. It is not known if it is intentional or not, but it seems to be often unintentional. In that case, it is not a lie. It is generally associated with frontal brain lobe dysfunction.[36] However, "normal" people often believe in contradictory things or without evidence or proof.

3. Factitious disorder (or faking). Patients who cannot stop from faking illnesses. They seem to have no reason for doing so. For example, a patient complains of back pain until admitted to a hospital. There is no evidence of back pain found. The patient may try also to have a number of unnecessary operations. (Also like munchausen syndrome.)

4. Machiavellianism. Psychologists often use this word in place of "lying." It derives from Machiavelli's **The Prince.** The Prince used lying to achieve his goals. (See R. Christie 1970).

5. Malingering. The person is often normal but fakes an illness, excuse, or reason in order to avoid work or punishment. Unlike factitious disorders, it is for a purpose.

6. Munchausen syndrome. Telling tall tales. It derives from the tall stories told by Baron Von Münchhausen. Usually it refers to faking an illness so as to be constantly hospitalized. (Hospital addiction, or "hospital hoboes.") See "factitious disorder" above.

7. Mythomania. An abnormal tendency to lie, create myths or exaggerate.

8. Pathological liar. One whose lies are so habitual, exaggerated and strange that it suggests a

disorder. But no one seems to have located a lie-disorder as such. Lying is not clearly a disease.

9. Pseudo-. From the Greek this means "false" or a lie. A number of words are created beginning with pseudo-, e.g., *pseudologia fantastica* is extravagant lying, often temporary.

VI. Truth

"Truths are illusions." Nietzsche

"No one has ever been truthful about what truthfulness is." Nietzsche

"Truth is a bare minimum or illusory idea." John Austin, philosopher

A. Oaths

In the courtroom, witnesses swear to "tell the truth, the whole truth and nothing but the truth so help me God." They sometimes lie anyway. Sometimes they ask to take another oath: "I swear to tell the truth, the whole truth and nothing but the truth on penalty of perjury." This oath is for non-religious witnesses.

There is a lot wrong with these oaths:

1. Taking an oath (merely saying one will tell the truth) does not guarantee that one will not lie.

Also, we saw that one may tell the truth by accident, and by lying. That is, one cannot take an oath to tell the objective truth, only the subjective truth.

2. "The truth" is an obscure and vague term. It can mean many things. It sometimes means, "That is good," "I agree," "That is correct," "He is faithful (true) to me," "That is accurate," "That is consistent," "That is not self-contradictory," etc.

When one speaks of "the Truth" it is not clear what is being said. The truth about what? What kind of truth? We do not know. There is no such thing as truth in itself. And if we are told that we will be given the truth today we do not know what we will be given. "The Truth" is not a thing.

"The truth" often refers merely to one's belief. H.L. Mencken, the American editor, put it this way:

> The truth that survives is simply the lie that is pleasantest to believe.

Also, what makes a lie is not objective truth, but belief. We cannot be asked to tell the truth if we do not know it. Thus, we should substitute "belief" for "truth" in the courtroom oath. The revised oath would read, "Tell your belief, your whole belief and nothing but your belief . . ."

3. Furthermore, no one could tell the "whole truth" about anything. We cannot know the whole

truth. We can always learn more about a matter. So we should not be asked to tell the "whole truth."

In addition, in the courtroom, the witness is usually asked to only answer the questions asked and to say no more. Thus, the witness is not even allowed to tell the whole story or "whole truth." In these ways we could not tell the truth even if we wanted to.

A statement is sometimes true and sometimes false. It is not always true. "It is raining," is true only when and where it is raining. If a "fact" in science is a statement which is "always true," there would be no facts in science. Facts are merely well-supported hypotheses or theories. Further evidence and observations may alter facts. Scientific facts are changing regularly. The great philosopher-scientist, Albert Einstein, states, "If you are out to describe the truth, leave elegance to the tailor."

If lies are untruths and there is no complete truth, then there is no complete lie either. This is one reason why the philosopher, Nietzsche, said that there is truth in falsity and falsity in truth. And to try to avoid being caught in a lie, people often tell lies which have a great deal of truth to them. If we cannot tell the complete truth, we cannot tell a complete lie either. But often a lie is as complete as we would ever need it to be.

B. Should We Always Tell the Truth?

> When in doubt, tell the truth. It will confound your enemies and astound your friends. (Mark Twain, *Pudd'nhead Wilson's New Calendar)*

We are told to "always tell the truth." What would happen if we did? We would hurt people's feelings or be tactless. We would say truthful things such as:

1. "You have just cooked the worst meal I have ever eaten."

2. "How did your operation go? I have never seen you look so horrible."

3. "You are probably the worst date I have ever had."

4. When asked, you tell a murderer where your friend is hiding.

5. "Your clothes are like dishrags."

We can be too truthful.

D. Bonhoeffer (1964) wrote,

> The truth can kill. . . . It is only the cynic who claims 'to speak the truth' at all times and in all places to all men in the same way. (pp. 363-372)

It is honesty humor to say what you are really thinking when most people would keep it secret.

You admit that you have a low intelligence and were the least popular person in your school. This reply is often unexpected and disappoints the one criticizing or calling names.

Philosophers and critical thinkers are more intellectually honest than most because they demand proof. They tell what they believe to be true even if people do not like what they hear.

The British essayist William Hazlitt wrote,

> There is nothing more likely to drive a man mad than an obstinate constitutional preference of the true to the agreeable.

One researcher, Max Weber, wrote,

> The primary task of a useful teacher is to teach his [or her] students to recognize "inconvenient facts—I mean facts that are inconvenient for their party opinions.

The philosopher Socrates was condemned to death for his critical and honest inquiry. People do not like to have their strong and favorite beliefs questioned. Philosophers and scientists usually defend honest, open, informed, critical inquiry even if it makes them unpopular with most people. Some of the greatest scientists and thinkers have been put to death for expressing their honest beliefs based on scientific research. This is what the critical and questioning philosopher, Nietzsche, called the "evil-eye" of the philosopher. It is the honest, questioning, critical eye.

To be uncritical of one's beliefs may be the most harmful form of dishonesty. Indoctrination, censorship, bias, prejudice all oppose honest, critical inquiry.

VII. Consequences of Lying

It was argued earlier that a lie is in itself not good or bad. It is just expressing other than what you believe. It is a lie whether or not the consequences are harmful or helpful.

A lie may cause harm and/or benefit to oneself and/or others. That is, a lie may:

a. harm one or another or both
b. harm one and benefit another
c. harm or benefit no one
d. prevent harm to one and/or both
e. prevent benefit to one and/or both
f. benefit one or other or both
g. harm one and/or another with no benefit to either
h. hurt no one, but benefit someone
i. etc.

It is clear then that lies can be harmful, helpful, or both.

It would be strange for someone to tell a lie which harms both oneself as well as others and benefits no one. On the other hand, it would be strange not to tell a lie which benefits everyone and harms no one. We tend to think that lies are told only which benefit oneself while causing harm to others. That is not true.

> **Exercise:** Give examples of a lie which has each of the above consequences.

It can be difficult to determine what the consequences of telling a lie or telling the truth will be. Because telling the truth is sometimes harmful does not mean we should never tell the truth. We must consider carefully the consequences of lying.

Some consequences of lying are the following:

1. Lying, whether beneficial or harmful, gives false information about one's beliefs, and possibly about facts. The result is that:

    a. we gain faulty information on which to make decisions and choices.

    b. we fail to understand what or how the liar really thinks. If we tell what we really believe, we can find out if it is justifiable or not.

c. a false or faulty friendship may be established with the liar.

d. communication is blocked. We usually expect people to tell the truth when they speak. If we cannot believe what people say we may soon stop listening or talking. We will pay no attention to what people say. This is why some people only believe on the basis of your actions, not what you say.

A well-known example of this is Aesop's fable of the shepherd boy and the wolf. The boy was lonely and thought of a plan to have some excitement. He knew the villagers would help him if a wolf ever attacked his sheep. So he went to the village and cried, "Wolf! Wolf!" The plan worked. The villagers came running in excitement, but found no wolf. Nevertheless, some of them stopped to talk with the boy for a long time. Later on in the summer the boy played the trick again and found it very enjoyable. But not long after that a wolf did come and attack the sheep. The boy cried "Wolf! Wolf!" but no one listened, though he spoke the truth.

Communication broke down. Now everything the boy says would be thought to be untrustworthy. People would say, "Whatever you say, I will not believe you."

2. Lying destroys the listener's ability to reason properly. Being lied to, often has the same consequences as ignorance, or lack of education.

3. By lying we support the technique of lying. But a justified lie need not support the telling of an unjustified lie. Kant asks what would happen if everyone lied. Telling harmful lies would undermine society. Kant believes, "A lie always harms another person."

On the other hand, we can reverse Kant's view and ask, "What if everyone always told the truth?" The result could be disastrous. But that is only because people think it is rude, tactless, insulting or impolite to always say exactly what you think. On the other hand, we may wish to change society so we can be more honest about what we think.

Also, the question need not be, "What if everyone lied?", but "What if everyone told a harmful lie?" If everyone only told beneficial lies, it could be desirable.

In addition, there is a difference between always telling the truth and always telling what we believe.

4. Love relationships, as well as friendships, may be broken by lies. To tell a harmful lie to someone may be to say we do not care about them.

5. Telling some lies may be self-contradictory because:

a. You may obtain a *benefit* by producing what you believe is a *harm* which you do not want to produce. We often feel guilty when we lie. People find they have to confess to lies even years after they were told.

b. You may be found out and punished for lying. The risk is often much greater than the gain.

c. You encourage others to deceive you as well. You would live in a society which you would not like.

d. You often have much more to lose than to gain by lying.

e. A lie may benefit one in the short run, but be harmful in the long run.

f. One of the most important qualities of a person is communication. If we destroy that, we destroy a large part of ourselves. In this sense we cease to exist. We become characterized as a liar or as an honest person. A lie defines us.

6. In law, a criminal is often regarded as responsible for all of the consequences of breaking the law. It is often difficult to know in advance all of

the harmful consequences which may result from telling a lie. A harmless-seeming lie may cause a death. To say your brother was home when he was not may cause him to be accused of a crime.

7. We may become used to lying.

8. If we lie about one fact, we often have to lie about other facts to cover up the first lie. One lie leads to another. Walter Scott wrote:

> Oh! What a tangled web we weave
> When first we practice to deceive.

9. If we know someone lies to us sometimes, it can cause anxiety. We do not feel secure or at ease with a liar.

10. When you lie, pretend you will be caught. How would you feel? Ask if you would do it again. Sometimes people know if we lie even as we tell the lie.

11. To be honest, it may be that most lies are never caught. We often only tell lies if we know no one will find them out. So, one of the reasons for not telling harmful lies is not punishment from others, but the fact that it is self-defeating. Possibly the main reason the philosopher, Kant, advises us never to lie is that it is self-contradictory to do so.

Shakespeare put it this way:

> This above all: to your own self be true,
> And it must follow, as the night the day,
> You cannot then be false to any man.
> (Hamlet)

A. Bluffing, Lying and Negotiation: A Case Example.

1. The Stereotype of Business as Unethical.

Business practices are held to involve everything from lying and exploitation to criminal activity. It makes "business ethics" appear like a contradiction in terms:

> Insofar as "business ethics" comes even close to ethics, it comes close to casuistry and will, predictably, end up . . . as special pleading for the powerful and the wealthy. (Drucker 1983, p. 39)

> The files . . . are filled with records of respectable companies that have not hesitated to break or stretch the law when they believed they could get away with it. (Carr 1983a, p. 30)

> Our mutual intent has *never* wavered—to gain an advantage over the other by means of deception. (Michelman 1983, p. 261)

Business is blamed and singled out for being unethical. I wish to at once and for all dispel this as a myth for four reasons: (1) the same abuses which apply in business apply elsewhere. It is not there alone. This is not, however, a *tu quoque* or "you also" justification. (2) The business establishment has as little knowledge about ethics and ethical theories as most other elements of society. Business ethics is a recent discipline, in some sense only getting underway in the 1980's, for example, the **Journal of Business Ethics.** G. Benson (1982) in his business ethics book wrote of "the United States, a country that largely ignores basic ethical instruction . . ." (p. 218) If we do not require ethics in our schools we cannot expect it in our companies. (3) To blame bakes no bread. It is to say that a past activity is bad. But (a) "bad" is a vague term, (b) we cannot change the past, (c) punishment for the past is mere retribution or, plainly put, revenge. In place of retaliatory blame or retribution, I recommend rehabilitative blame. That is, the only value of blame is either to determine a cause, or to attempt to change behavior in the future. In this sense, blame is a retreat to the future. Thus, business practice need not be blamed except insomuch as such practices can be corrected. Business itself is not the enemy and not to be blamed as such. (4) We cannot generalize about all or even most business practices being abuses. This would be a fallacy of oversimplification.

2. *Ethics in Business: Is Business Ethics Special?*

Business is thought to have a special ethics of its own such that it need not follow the moral principles of society. It is thought to be, in Nietzsche's phrase, "beyond good and evil." The other institution of this sort we usually call "crime."

> Business operates with a special code of ethics. (Carr 1983, p. 24)

Would this mean that every institution of society would also have an ethics of its own? I will, in the following, support and expand Drucker's (1983) statement, "there is only one ethics . . ." (p. 32)

A model for clarifying ethics is as follows. The ethical theory chosen here is a descriptive one according to which ethical terms (basically: good-bad, should-should not, right-wrong) and their synonyms are open-context terms with a loosely limited range of substitution instances. (Shibles 1972) "Responsibility" and "duty" reduce to "should" or "ought." A descriptive statement is distinguished from a value (moral or ethical) statement by the use of such open-context terms. Any descriptive statement can be transformed into a value statement by the addition of such terms. For example, "The prices were stable," is descriptive. "The prices were bad," is a value statement.

Carson's (1982) phrase, "moral goodness and the moral virtue," (p. 20) is circular and redundant because "moral" is a synonym of both "good" and "virtue."

In themselves, ethical terms are meaningless, as the Positivists had concluded—but for different reasons. To say, "Your action was bad," is like saying, "Your action was X." In order to know what "The price-fixing is wrong," means, we must substitute something for "wrong." It could mean (a) "bad." "It is wrong because it is bad," is circular. (b) There is too much (value term) price-fixing. (circular) (c) There should (value term) be more price-fixing. (Circular and contradicts b) (d) It opposes the majority. (Appeal-to-the-majority fallacy) (e) It is illegal. (Appeal to authority) (f) It violates social custom. (Relativism) (g) It is not usually done. (Argument from tradition) (h) It is unusual. (Argument from familiarity)

"Bad," like other ethical terms, is a general term. It is empty. It is like a blank check, or "X" in algebra, a function admitting of variables. The director who says, "I *favor progress* for this corporation," has not yet said anything. The advertisement slogan, "Soup is *good* food," is as empty as an unfilled can. "You are to blame (bad)," is in itself unintelligible.

We, thus, not only cannot intelligibly say that

"price-fixing is in itself wrong or blameworthy," but also *a fortiori* because no substitution is specified, and some instances are contradictory. To assert that anything is bad (or good) or blameworthy in itself, is a misuse of ethical terms.

Any theory of ethics must account for the fact that ethical terms are among the most confusing and abused terms in our language. Thus, business people are justifiably confused about them also. This confusion is accounted for by the descriptive observation that many if not most of the substitution usages, as illustrated above (a-h), are informal logical fallacies.

If the fallacies and circularities are to be circumvented, not only can ethical terms be reduced to naturalistic terms, but they must do so if ethical terms are to be made intelligible. We must accordingly revise our language to cohere with a naturalistic theory. Business is misled in ethics by the very language we speak. John Dewey's naturalistic ethics would be a model of the above sort of naturalistic theory. Definitions of ethical terms must be in terms of non-ethical terms to avoid circularity. There is no fallacy involved in doing so.

A naturalistic ethics would, generally speaking, reduce "good" to bringing about our deliberately chosen wants and likes in the context of our knowledge of consequences in a rational, noncontradictory way. This is an enlightened egoism, not selfishness or a mere profit-motive ethics, because bringing about one's wants involves political and social wants as well. At any specified moment what we mean by "wrong," roughly, is "I do not want it in terms of what I know about it." A naturalistic ethics is simultaneously a theory of meaning and an argument (serves a reason-giving function).

The ability to be ethical requires increasing inquiry into consequences, emotion, ethical language, and the improvement of knowledge and communication generally. Carr (1983a) reflects this position as follows:

> Nonethical practice is shortsighted almost by definition . . . I would go so far as to say that almost anything an executive does, on whatever level, to extend the range of thinking of his superiors tends to effect an ethical advantage. (p. 31)

The use of the words "ethical advantage" is well-chosen. Also, on the naturalistic view, any dogmatic (e.g., religious) belief system would be immoral. Religious systems and values are highly criticized as well from the point of view of most ethical theories whether by Dewey's naturalistic theory or not (e.g., Kant's ethics). Thus, the following statements by Carr (1983) which suggest that ethics be grounded on religion, are inappropriate:

> No one expects poker to be played on the ethical principles preached in churches. (p. 20)
>
> The ethics of business are game ethics, different from the ethics of religion. (p. 20)

The ethics of business is now seen to be no different than ethics anywhere else. Ethics is just the use of open-context ethical terms and such terms are used everywhere and everyday. There is no monopoly on the use of ethical language.

3. Profit as the Ethical Standard

Adam Smith (1937) held that the prime drive in economic man is self-interest, but he also spoke of enlightened self-interest not mere selfishness. This, to some extent, coheres with the enlightened egoism presented in the last section. If I am to achieve my wants adequately as a full human being I must also be concerned about others and society in a humane and caring way.

In ethics, the goals are to be determined not by a single want alone, but by an enlightened, adequate harmony of all of one's wants and desires. Following the economic theory it is usually assumed that the goal of business is monolithic: to maximize profits. Clearly this would not suffice as a goal for an ethical system. The appropriation of ethics by economics has led to the sterotype of business as basically unethical:

> If by "conscience" he meant a sense of right and wrong transcending the economic, he was asking the impossible. (Carr 1983a, p. 29)

> Assuming the profit maximizing goals for each, deception often seems to be an unavoidable characteristic of negotiation. (Michelman 1983, p. 256)

The result of the profit motive as an end in itself is dehumanization and poverty in regard to the quality of our lives, whether one be an executive or worker. An analogy brings out the absurdity. Consider a marriage or friendship based merely on the profit motive. There would be no longer a reason to have such relationships because one's wants would no longer be satisfied in an adequate way.

The Nobel economist Paul Samuelson who wrote perhaps the most used economics text, denied that an "invisible hand" will somehow result from each individual seeking their own profit alone:

> In short, Adam Smith . . . had no right to assert that an Invisible Hand channels individuals selfishly seeking their own interests into promoting the 'public

> interest' . . . . Smith has proved nothing of this kind, nor has any economist or philosopher since his time. (p. 574) (cf. Johnson 1985)

Smith, however, is said to have used the term "invisible hand" once, and besides his claim was only that seeking self interest frequently, not always, can result in the promotion of the interest of society. (Barry 1983, p. 50)

John Dewey argued similarly that the *laissez-faire* view of Adam Smith is outmoded, that planning is instead needed. Dewey argued that the "invisible hand" idea is sheer myth. Selfishness is by definition, self-contradictory. Profit may be a necessary condition for a business but it is not a sufficient condition.

4. Legality as the Ethical Standard

When Socrates asked the statesman what justice was, the latter replied that it was acting in accord with the laws of the state. Socrates quickly pointed out that we change the laws of the state and therefore that cannot be the standard. Nevertheless, we find business treating the law as the substitution instance for open-context ethical terms:

> As long as they comply with the letter of the law, they are within their rights to

> operate their businesses as they see fit. (Carr 1983, p. 21)

Here "right" means "obey the law."

> As long as a company does not transgress the rules of the game set by law, it has the legal right to shape its strategy without reference to anything but its profits. (Carr 1983, p. 22)

> The decision-making process at top-management levels has little room for social responsibilities not definitely required by law or public opinion. (Carr 1983a, p. 28)

"The letter of the law" and "the spirit of the law" differ. The "letter of the law" may refer to what is defeasible (how a case will hold up in court). The spirit of the law refers to what is humanistic and in the interests of public welfare. In this second meaning the above typical quotations show that there is usually no concern by business for the spirit of the law, and furthermore their actions may sometimes be illegal.

> Agreements to do immoral or unethical acts violate the public welfare and are illegal. (Fiber & Weigle 1983, p. 85)

5. Bluffing, Lying and Negotiation

Much recent literature on the subject of bluffing and lying in business supports these practices as in some sense acceptable practices:

> A great deal of lying and deception . . . is openly condoned or encouraged by both business and labor. (Carson 1982, p. 20)

> Many forms of bluffing in labor negotiations are legal . . .(Carson 1982, p. 13)

It is not clear that bluffing and lying are as legal as it is suggested. Sections 8(a)(5) and 8(b)3 of the National Labor Relations Act state that both the union and employer must bargain "in good faith." "Good faith" is taken to mean that any material claims made must be honest claims. (Carson 1982, p. 13)

In any case, businesses could lie even if it is illegal, if they are not concerned about the penalty. In that case, presumably, businesses can and should break the law when it is to their advantage and/or the profit motive will be satisfied.

Why should lying be so liberally allowed even where it is not illegal? In daily life, lying is not usually acceptable. In the discussions of lying, a definition of lying is not given except for the article by Carson (1982). However, even there, contradictory analyses are presented. Before dealing with bluffing and lying in negotiation, a model of lying must be presented.

"Bluff" derives from Dutch "bluffen" meaning to boast, or play a kind of card game. It means to deceive, to trick; to frighten, or deter by threat, pretense or mere show of strength. On this analysis, to bluff is a form of force, extortion, or deception, all of which are irrational and forms of informal logical fallacies. They do not involve inquiry, sound argument, or good communication.

Bluffing is treated as meaning, lying. The previously given definition of lying showed that they are different.

In view of the new definition of lying, the following asertions are unacceptable:

> A lie is a deliberate false statement intended to deceive another person. (Carson 1982, p. 16)

> Bluffing typically does not amount to lying. (Carson 1982, p. 18)

If nothing is expressed or said, bluffing is not lying. If it is, bluffing is lying, but it is also in addition an intent to deceive.

Perhaps one could also bluff without intending to deceive.

> Lying always involves the intent to deceive others . . . (Carson 1982, p. 18)

This is in direct opposition to the new theory of lying.

> There is no presumption against bluffing or deceiving someone who is attempting to bluff or deceive you on that occasion. (Carson 1982, p. 19)

This is a *tu quoque* or "you also" fallacy. The article also states that in negotiations we presume the opponent is lying unless we have evidence to the contrary. Lying, therefore, has the consequences of undermining trust in business generally as a presumption. It should be pointed out that the Carson (1982) article shows more insight than most other accounts of lying, and agrees in a number of points with the new theory.

Some other questionable justifications given of lying in negotiations are common enough so that, in the main, no special sources need be cited:

a. Lying is allowed because only the profit-motive is important.

b. Business need not concern itself with being humanistic.

c. An executive will lose salary, prestige or the executive position if she or he does not lie. (For the same reason one may argue that we should support the prevailing prejudices of the community (e.g. racial and gender prejudice). This, of course, would not be acceptable.)

d. It is a matter of survival of the fittest.

e. That is just the way the game is played. (Carr 1983, pp. 24, 20) (This can also be said about anything.)

f. We should use every trick to win.

g. Bluffing should force and pressure the other into concessions.

h. We should distort and conceal information for our own advantage regardless of the disadvantage of the other.

i. Lying is necessary, faced with the realities of a harsh market place.

In the first place, lying is not wrong in itself, but only when the consequences are harmful. If lying is harmful in everyday life, it is also harmful in business. This is to oppose Carr (1983):

> No one should think any the worst of the game of business because its standards of right and wrong differ from the prevailing traditions of morality in our society. (p. 20)

Lying in negotiations does not create a pretty picture. The consequences of harmful lying are:

a. Communication is undermined.

b. Vital interests may be ignored.

c. It can be unhumanistic.

d. It involves informal logical fallacies such as deception, force, concealment of information, appeal to emotions.

e. Both parties lack the needed information and communication necessary to reach a settlement.

f. An atmosphere of enmity is created thereby making everyone's job unpleasant. If the point of the negotiation is to improve the quality of one's life, the lying and bluffing undermines that goal and so is self-defeating.

g. Lying and bluffing are often short-term gains only. By their use, one wins the battle but loses the war.

h. In ordinary life if a person lies and bluffs we would reject that person from our lives.

i. If an employer lies in negotiations an employee may well lie in her or his job all the rest of the time. No one can be depended on any longer.

j. Harmful lying undermines our business, law, social life, society and political system.

k. Profit is not the only reasonable goal to be negotiated, thus lying to maximize profit may undermine other goals.

Basically, unjustified lying and bluffing undermine the very negotiation process, communication and the quality of the lives of the human beings involved. In short, it is self-defeating in the long or short run. It leads to increased governmental controls, legislation, consumer protection action, unions, etc. (The 1970's have seen increase of such societal controls, including, of course, the work of the Ralph Nader forces.) If employees do not know if increased wage demands will in fact force bankruptcy, they may (and have recently) force companies out of business.

If there are no facts, is no trustworthy information, no spirit of concern for the interests of all and society, negotiations serve only to break down negotiations. It is self-defeating, self-lie and life-lie. And this is to express a view of Socrates, that because it is self-contradictory, we only do harm out of ignorance:

> No one voluntarily does wrong, but that all who do wrong do so against their own will. (**Gorgias** 509e, **Meno, Timaeus**)

Several writers on business ethics have reflected a similar viewpoint:

> Once trained in self-criticism and self-monitoring, there will be less harm done out of ignorance. (Oelschlaeger 1981)

> The better his reputation for integrity, honesty, and decency, the better his chances of victory will be in the long run. (Carr 1983, p. 24)

It would be as metaphysical to assert that honesty alone will succeed, as that *laissez-faire* capitalism or the profit-motive in itself will succeed. What is concluded is that we should adopt a consequentialistic, naturalistic ethics, deliberately choose our wants and likes; and use informed, adequate inquiry and communication in order to bring about these goals. Business transactions and negotiations are not immune from the practicality and effectiveness of such a rational approach.

SOURCES

Barry, Vincent. *Moral Issues in Business* CA: Wadsworth 1983.

Benson, George. *Business Ethics in America* MA: Heath 1982.

Carr, Albert. "Can an Executive Afford a Conscience?" in Barry 1983a, *op. cit.* Reprinted from *Harvard Business Review July-Aug. 1970.*

Carr, Albert. "Is Business Bluffing Ethical?" in V. Barry 1983. Reprinted from *Harvard Business Review* Jan-Feb 1968.

Carson, T., Wokutch, R., Murrman, K. "Bluffing in Labor Relations: Legal and Ethical Issues." *Journal of Business Ethics* 1 (Fall 1982) 13-22.

Drucker, Peter. "Ethical Chic." in Barry 1983. Reprinted from *Forbes* Sept. 14, 1981.

Fiber, Larry & Weigle, Jerry. *Applied Business Law* VA: Reston Publishing 1983.

Michelman, James. "Deception in Commercial Negotiation." *Journal of Business Ethics* 2(4) (Nov. 1983) 255-262.

Oelschlaeger, Max. "Philosophical Therapy for Business Managers." *Southwest Philosophical Studies* 6(1981) 98-104.

Shibles, Warren. "Ethics as Open-Context Terms." in *Philosophical Pictures* IA: Kendall-Hunt 1972.

Smith, Adam. *An Inquiry into the Nature and Causes of the Wealth of Nations* NY: Random House 1937.

B. Truth and Lying in Advertising: A Case Example

> Many a small thing has been made large by the right kind of advertising. (Mark Twain)

As a result of widespread lying and deception in advertising:

1. In Sweden, there are no commercials on radio or television. (Also because of government control.)

2. In Germany, one political party *(Die Grünen)* advocates banning advertising and replacing it with making easily available true, accurate, objective information about each product or service. The product or service would have to be

first approved for its effect on safety, reliability, ecology, society, etc.

3. In the United States, numerous organizations had to be created which regulate advertising. (Federal Communications Commission (FCC), Federal Trade Commission (FTC), Food and Drug Administration (FDA), etc.) They attempt to ensure truth in advertising and to ensure that products are labeled correctly, include accurate descriptions of ingredients and amounts, and that full information be given including warnings regarding misuse or harmful substances.

4. In addition to other controls, advertisers themselves have seen a need to make advertising more truthful and they have voluntarily created their own code and agencies of self-regulation (e.g., National Advertising Review Board, TV Code Review Board, etc.).

The consequences of lying and deception in advertising have resulted in lack of credibility, increased laws and restrictions on advertisers, as well as more strict liability for manufacturers.

In addition, a vocabulary of lying has been developed to identify the kind of lie or deception the advertiser uses: false promises, claims of uniqueness (saying that a product is "unique" or "unparalleled"), incomplete description, misleading comparisons, bait and switch offers (advertise a sale item to attract the customer, then say it is sold out and "switch" them to a more expensive item), visual distortion, testimonials, false comparison, superlative words (e.g., "the finest," "the greatest"), partial disclosures, small-print qualifications, underselling claims (e.g., "lowest prices in town"), etc. (Bovée and Arens 1982) (p. 59)

The Creative Code of the American Association of Advertising Agencies states:

> We will not knowingly produce advertising which contains:
>
> a. False or misleading statements or exaggerations, visual or verbal.
> b. Testimonials which do not reflect the real choice of a competent witness.
> c. Price claims which are misleading.
> d. Comparisons which unfairly disparage a competitive product or service.
> e. Claims insufficiently supported, or which distort the true meaning or practicable application of statements made by professional or scientific authority.
> f. Statements, suggestions, or pictures offensive to public decency.
> g. Excessive repetition.

In addition to the vocabulary of lying above, we are presented with this code which lists the ways in which advertisers sometimes lie and deceive. To this we may add logical criteria. Do advertisements violate rational arguments? Do they commit the informal logical fallacies such as appeal to the majority, appeal to fear, contradiction, circularity, false cause, false analogy, appeal to ignorance, etc.?

One of the main goals of advertising is to "communicate information about the product." (Bovée and Arens 1982, p. 45) To communicate objective information the logical fallacies should not be committed. Otherwise advertising would be mere indoctrination and deception. Repetition, for instance, is a form of indoctrination.

A look at a few contemporary advertisements chosen at random will determine how well the codes and government regulations have succeeded. ("O" refers to the fallacy of the use of open-context ethical terms.)

a. "America's favorite bran flakes." (O) (Also appeal to majority.)

b. "Soup is good food." (O) (Also empty of content. It says only that soup is food. It is circular in that "soup" partly means "food." Compare "Water is wet." "Food" only means that one can eat it.

c. "Made of the finest fiber . . . Delicious Bean with Bacon Soup." (O) (The reader is led to believe there is "finest" fiber as opposed to other "worst" fiber. No evidence or clarification is given.

d. The following mouthwash advertisement will be analyzed in terms of its history:

> Listerine advertised for 50 years as a germ killer . . . Readers were admonished to gargle Listerine quick! The FTC held in the 1970s that the product did not relieve colds or sore throats and forced the company to include a corrective statement which said that the product was of no value in preventing colds and sore throats. (Bovée and Arens 1982, p. 65)

It has been pointed out that mouthwashes even upset the equilibrium of the mouth, do not reach the sore throat, are caused often by a virus which is not killed but requires antibiotics, dries up the mucous membranes, may delay a needed examination by a physician, etc. (Graedon 1976, pp. 92-96).

Zimmerman's **The Essential Guide to Non-prescription Drugs** (1983), gives the following descriptions of mouthwashes as false or misleading: (p. 686)

> promotes flow of saliva
> antimicrobial cleansing action
> quiets rasping cough due to colds which may be causing discomfort
> healing aid
> relieves dryness
> soothing to smoker's throat
> acts fast (time can't be demonstrated)
> fast healing aid
> kills germs in minutes

long-lasting relief
quick comfort to irritated throats
for temporary relief of pain associated with canker sores (medical diagnosis should be made)
temporary relief of pain of stomatitis
relieves pain due to tonsillitis
helps kill mouth germs
healing aid for minor oral inflammation

Asperheim and Eisenhauer (1973) write in **The Pharmacologic Basis of Patient Care:**

> Gargles and mouthwashes . . . are often highly overrated in advertisements, however; they are usually only weakly medicated and cannot be depended upon to correct bad breath, heal mouth lesions, cure sore throats or perform the many other health-preserving effects for which they are promoted. (p. 374)

We may keep this in mind in reading the following 1984 advertisement:

> THE
> INVISIBLE
> ENEMY
>
> Plaque
>
> . . . today, we have clinical evidence to show that the same old Listerine Antiseptic that for so many years has been killing the germs that cause bad breath also kills something else: the germs that cause plaque buildup. While brushing

> alone can of course remove plaque, Listerine can get to places even your toothbrush can't. So with a professional cleaning, regular brushing, and rinsing with Listerine twice a day, you can reduce plaque buildup up to 50% over brushing alone . . . It's really that simple . . . A very important weapon . . . Good old Listerine.

Some of the fallacies produced here are as follows:

1. Scare tactics and fallacy of force are used in reference to "The invisible enemy"!

2. The product kills germs but "germs" is also a negative value term here. Graedon (1976) argued that it is harmful to kill germs in this way.

3. It is blatant vice to refer to "old" and "good old" Listerine, when they deceived readers for over fifty years.

4. The claim that Listerine kills bad breath is a false cause fallacy and fallacy of abstractionism. "Bad breath" is a symptom, a vague term, and not a medical disorder as such. It may be caused by infection, tooth decay, lung or liver disease, garlic (which enters the blood stream and lungs), etc., none of which can be corrected by mouth washes. "Killing the germs that cause bad breath" could mean only that it kills a relatively few of the billions of germs, or kills only the same *type* of germ which causes bad breath. The same applies to plaque germs.

5. We are not told how or what evidence there is that Listerine reduces plaque.

6. The logician would have a field day with the statement, "So with professional cleaning, regular brushing, and rinsing with Listerine twice a day, you can reduce plaque buildup by up to 50% over brushing alone . . ." This statement could possibly be true if we substituted water for Listerine. Statistical vagueness is contained in this use of 50%.

e. "It's worth going out of your way for." (O)

f. "Chicken is always better with a little . . . olé." (olives) (All-fallacy, Open-context value comparison.)

g. Mennen: "Creme can help keep your skin smooth." "Help" can be vague. With "help" an automobile could also fly to the moon. Also, black tar or honey could help make one's skin appear smooth.

h. "Jell-O Frozen Snacks: Lots of Taste." Castor oil and bitter fruit also have "lots of taste."

i. Shade Sunscreen Lotion: "Nothing gives you better sunburn protection." This could mean that nothing at all gives one better protection. Couldn't not going in the sun give one better protection?

j. "Sweet 'N Low the most used diet product ever." First of all, the package indicates that it may cause cancer. Secondly, it commits the fallacy of appeal to majority. Thirdly, it is hard to substantiate. Is water a more used diet product?

k. "The future calls for Culligan" (water softeners). A vague claim. What does the future call for Culligan for? What does it say to Culligan?

l. "natural ingredients." Even poisons can be natural.

m. Feen-a-mint Laxative Pills: "For gentle and predictable relief." Graedon (1976) says to stay away from this one. Such laxatives can harm the intestinal machinery. (p. 327)

n. "More than 7 out of 10 women surveyed preferred new Curél over therapeutic Keri lotion. They told us it was better . . ." (O) (Appeal to majority fallacy. Unscientifically presented and incomplete information. Based on mere opinion.)

o. "The medicine in Bufferin goes into your bloodstream fast and works where you hurt to quickly relieve minor arthritis pain." This advertisement is, perhaps, honest in stating that it applies to "minor" pain. It also adds "Use only as directed." On the other hand, Graedon (1976) claims that "This is a good way to die unexpectedly," that it irritates the stomach which may lead to an ulcer and it thins the blood which improves the chances for a hemorrhage.

p. Automobile advertisement: "Takes you where you want to go." This is interesting. In one sense it is circular. If I want to go one mile, it will take me one mile. What would the alternative be? Perhaps it will stall as I drive away. Or if I wish to go to Chicago, perhaps the car I drive will take me to New York: "But I didn't want to go to New York." Perhaps this car is for people who say in fear, "I wonder where my car will take me today?"

Certainly some advertisements are circular but yet entertain or try to draw attention to practical and simple auto construction. The Volkswagen company showed a moon vehicle with the caption: "It's ugly but it gets you there." But then it also advertised the VW "Bug" as being a car which goes forward and backwards. In their modesty they did not even state that the car had doors through which one could enter and leave the car. The advertisements of VW have been brilliant in terms of their humor.

q. Many advertisements use metaphor and fantasy to create moods, or even to sell images. Perfume, clothes, jewelry, are several products using this technique. An examination of such language is of special interest in understanding the boundaries of truth and lie. Consider also True cigarettes: "This True we like"; More cigarettes: "Dare to be more." If one develops cancer one will be more. Honesty, would rather suggest the names "Lie cigarettes," "Cancer cigarettes," or simply "Death cigarettes." The military advises, "Be all that you can be." In battle one can be killed.

The reader must draw her or his own conclusions about truth in advertising as it now exists. It is clear, however, that it regularly commits logical fallacies, deviates from the advertiser's code, and is far from being honest and without deceit. The consequences affect the life, health, safety and satisfaction of the consumer.

Exercise:

Examine advertisements to see if they are misleading, violate advertising codes or are illogical.

SOURCES

Asperheim, Mary; Eisenhauer, Laurel. *The Pharmacologic Basis of Patient Care* 2nd ed. PA: Saunders 1973

Bovée, Courtland and Arens, W. *Contemporary Advertising* IL: R. Irwin 1982.

Graedon, Joe. *The People's Pharmacy* N.Y.: St. Martin's Press 1976.

Zimmerman, David. *The Essential Guide to Nonprescription Drugs* N.Y.: Harper & Row 1983

VIII. Why Do We Lie?

Everyone tells lies of one sort or another, so the question is not "Do we lie?", but "Why do we lie?"

The most common beliefs are that we lie:

1. out of selfishness to obtain something we want.

2. to avoid being punished or blamed.

There are many other reasons for lying which we tend not to be aware of. We lie:

3. for social reasons and to be polite. Some have signed letters, "Your obedient servant." I doubt if such people would be so obedient as to mow our grass and clean our house. There is a sense in which social lying is anti-social.

4. out of habit.

5. as a joke. We tell "tall" stories or exaggerate to create humor. Humor is produced when the person knows it is a lie and accepts the telling of the lie.

6. to indoctrinate into some fixed belief.

7. to help people who are in trouble.

8. because others around us lie.

9. because we are forced to.

10. to avoid unfairness.

11. to protect or help continue other people's false but comfortable beliefs.

12. to avoid embarrassment.

13. because we are irrational or not thinking clearly.

14. because we fail to understand the harm of lying.

15. because we do not wish to tell our private beliefs.

16. because of a mutual agreement to lie about certain things. A person may request to be told she will live a long life even if she knows she may not. Many, if not most, people do not want to know exactly when and how they will die. We may want to be flattered even if it is not true.

17. for convenience. We put an "out to lunch" sign on the office door even when we are not actually planning to eat. We just do not have another sign handy.

18. because we take it to be a "white lie." We may lie if we think the matter is quite unimportant and it would not matter whether or not we were found out. You say you left at 10 p.m., when you really left at 10:02. However, "white lies" may be extremely important, such as in a murder trial. Here, many small details may be used to solve the crime. We cannot know in advance how important the consequences of a "white lie" will turn out to be.

19. because we are unsure what is meant. We may say, "I will always love you," without knowing what is involved in such a promise. We are not sure whether we believe it or not.

20. out of carelessness or inaccuracy. We say we "cannot" do something, when we mean that we do not want to. We say we *need* something, when it is really a *want* or *desire.*

21. as a quick way of saying something to avoid lengthy discussion.

22. to avoid facing facts or reality—a cowardly lie.

23. to get revenge.

24. because we are encouraged to agree.

25. to escape from or avoid the truth. We may lie about the nature of death. These may be called "crucial lies."

26. as a boast, or to try to show superiority.

27. to protect someone from doing a foolish act.

28. because we think it is for someone's own good.

29. to pass an exam. You may not believe what you state, but know what is wanted on the test.

30. because in certain professions such as spying, we are trained to lie to accomplish the task. Detectives or military interrogators may lie to obtain information.

31. for no clear reason. Certain disturbed people cannot seem to stop lying. Some are called "pathological liars." Anyone may lie without knowing why he or she lies. A lie is a lie even if we have no motive or reason for telling it. In law, a motive is not needed to find one guilty of perjury.

32. not to mislead. We may lie because we know the other person will believe the opposite of what we say.

33. to achieve a goal. This raises the question of whether the means justifies the ends.

34. to produce irony. (Saying the opposite of what we believe.)

35. to help a patient feel better and so return to health more rapidly.

36. to create excitement and avoid boredom. This was the case with the shepherd who cried "wolf."

37. to an irrational or disturbed person to prevent serious harm.

38. to keep up team spirit as in "pep talks."

39. to show what a lie is and to analyze lies for students.

40. because we are confused about what a lie is and not sure whether it is good or bad.

41. to protect our beliefs.

Now it is clear that it is a fallacy to say that the liar intends to mislead or do harm. People intend many different sorts of things when they lie. We have different motives for lying, some are the best, some are the worst. The kind of lying we do shows the kind of person we are.

We may lie to balance out wrongs done to us. We may not wish to be honest with one who will abuse the truth. It may seem justifiable to lie to someone who is unfair to us or lied to us. It may be our only way of "evening the score." But such lies would have to be justified as would any other. It is not enough to say we can lie to someone who has no "right" to the truth. "Right" is a vague term which first needs clarification.

Lying should not be regarded as an "escape-valve." Rather we should organize our lives and resolve our conflicts so that lies are not required. If we know we cannot depend on lies as an ultimate refuge, we will rearrange our life with a new balance. It stresses prevention rather than cure. If we know we must tell the truth to a lover we will not be as tempted to violate a trust. The best lie is the lie that we did not have to tell. The balance that not lying provides, gives a harmony to life. It is an important factor in the creation of an aesthetic life.

IX. The Logic of Flattery: Beneficial Lying (An Exercise in Analysis)

"Lying is a necessity of life." Nietzsche

"You are very special." "You are the most desirable person I have ever met." "You are the most beautiful and intelligent person in the world." "I love only you."

We love flattery and seem to need it. Yet "flattery" is defined as false praise, insincere praise, pleasing deception, or excessive praise. Why do we seem to need to be lied to in this way?

We may turn to Shakespeare, a master of language, of rhetoric, of the logic of flattery and lying. His love sonnet is presented for analysis.

Sonnet #138

When my love swears that she is made
of truth,

I do believe her, though I know she lies,
That she might think me some untutor'd
youth,
Unlearned in the world's false subtleties.
Thus vainly thinking that she thinks
me young,
Although she knows my days are past
the best,
Simply I credit her false-speaking tongue:
On both sides thus is simple truth
suppress'd.
But wherefore says she not she is unjust?
And wherefore say not I that I am old?
O, love's best habit is in seeming trust,
And age in love loves not to have
years told:

Therefore I lie with her and she with me,
And in our faults by lies we flatter'd be.

He believes her lies because he knows that the lover's lie is a language-game, a technique of language in order to say subtle things. It is irony that we should purposefully believe a lie we know is a lie. But that is equivocation. We do not believe the lie. We believe what is intended by the lie. Both liar and the lover lied to, know that what is said is false. What the liar is saying by the lie is that she loves him and cares for him. That is love's truth. It is to use a lie to tell the truth about one's feelings. We love and desire the other person so much we lie for them. That is, an objective lie is told in order to present the subjective truth. And, as with humor, both lovers know it is a lie and thereby achieve the deepest feelings for one another.

Flattery here is a seeming lie which reveals some truth. The lie is that the lie is in fact subjective truth in disguise. And further, this suggests that our faults, which we take as objective truths, are lies and fictions, which rather have their own beauties and truths — the beauty of old age, and of a world we can only partially understand, or the beauty in the idea that the worst people only do harm out of awkward attempts to do the best. We transform the fictions of the world.

By means of such flattery and lies our beautiful feelings for one another are shown to overcome the worst in life, to transcend death itself. Love conquers all.

We can never know if another can be trusted. It would destroy the relationship to be constantly checking on someone. So we develop the habit of "seeming trust." We take the attitude of trust even when we cannot with certainty know if there are violations. By so doing we create the love, and that is the point. The goal is achieved by taking the fiction of seeming trust. Flattery is tact and concern, to say the best and not the worst. The word "flattery" derives from "flatten" in the sense of "making even," "stroking," "caressing," in order to please.

And so the irony is that by seeming lies, we tell the truth about our love to create one of the greatest experiences we will ever know.

Flattery here is a seeming lie which reveals a truth. The lie is that the lie is in fact truth in disguise.

The paradox or seeming contradiction in riddle form is:

Q. How may we tell the truth by lying?
A. By flattery.

The lover wants to be regarded as the most beautiful person in the world. We now know why. It is not just to deny the truth about ourselves. It is to believe the truth that the lover accepts us, the subjective truth that in the lover's eyes we are unequalled. This subjective truth creates the truth. If someone thinks we are beautiful, we by that thought become beautiful. This flattery is not, then, a mere idealization or false belief. The lover's desire to be the best is well-founded. We create our love by our own attitudes and thoughts or statements.

There are at least several types of flattery. In the above, type I, an objective lie is told, but also a real, subjective or emotional truth is told. You say what you emotionally believe is true. You are true to your emotions. This may be called "genuine flattery."

Type II. Here, a subjective as well as an objective lie is told. With this type of flattery one lies both about the facts and about one's subjective feelings. This is "false flattery." **Webster's Dictionary** says this type of lie is told for the purpose of self-gain or for one's own benefit. But social lies or other "false flattery" may be used for beneficial purposes on certain occasions.

Type III. Flattery can be what is objectively true for most people, but subjectively false. You may say, "This is an excellent cake," and objectively, most people will think so, but you may dislike cake. It is not a contradiction to say, "This is an excellent cake, but I hate cake."

A friend or lover may sometimes want either the objective truth or the subjective truth, but it should be indicated which is desired. A careful and honest reply may be, "Most people will like this dress, although I prefer the green one."

X. Justifications for Lying

It was argued that a lie is not in itself good or bad. A good lie which helps everyone need not be justified. The question becomes, "How can we justify a harmful lie?"

We tend to blame only the person who tells the harmful lie. But if no one believes the lie there may be no harm done. So the believer is partly to blame for believing a lie. Charles Lamb, the English essayist, wrote, "Some people do not know what to do with truth when it is offered to them."

It is up to us to check out and be critical of what we are told. In advertising and business we say, "Let the buyer beware." The same applies to cases of lying. Beware that what you hear may be a lie. Trust your fellow card players, but always cut the deck.

In critical thinking we may even, at first, assume that it is possible that every statement is false or a lie. It needs to be tested, not believed blindly. There would be fewer liars if there were fewer uncritical believers.

Lying is often done out of ignorance. We have not been clever enough to solve our problems without lying.

Some say it is alright to lie to a child. H. Grotius, jurist and statesman, wrote, "It is permissible to say what is false before infants and insane persons."[3] But the statement is faulty. A lie is neither good nor bad in itself. It is alright to tell a beneficial lie to a child, but not alright to tell a harmful lie to a child. It is not alright to tell every kind of lie to a child or anyone else. The philosopher Bertrand Russell (1950) wrote:

> To tell lies to the young, who have no means of checking what they are told, is morally indefensible. (p. 21)

A. *How do we know whether or not to tell a beneficial lie—an "honest lie"?*

Here are some possible tests:

1. See if the problem can be solved without lying. It must be clear that there are no better alternatives than lying.

2. Ask if you would wish to be lied to in those circumstances.

3. Ask yourself if that person would wish to be lied to in these circumstances.

4. Ask the person if you should lie to her or him, before the lie is told. In some cases permission may be given in advance.

5. Investigate as thoroughly as possible to make sure the lie will produce more benefit than harm. Make sure your arguments and reasonings are sound.

6. Ask other informed people whether they also think a lie should be told in that case.

7. Determine whether your lie, if detected, would result in loss of trust and produce a greater harm.

8. Do the ends or goals justify the means (lying)?

B. *Some faulty excuses or justifications for harmful lying are:*

1. Lack of knowledge or understanding. We say, "I didn't know by lying that I would cause you to miss your flight."

2. If a person with power over us (employer, parent, judge, authority, police officer, etc.) is unfair, we may feel justified in lying to avoid the unfairness. This is not reason enough. The same tests for lying given above should first be considered. Otherwise we may also be charged with lying.

3. It may be unjustifiable to lie merely because someone lies to us. Because a child lies to us does not justify us in lying to the child.

4. We may lie for revenge. But "getting back" at someone is merely to do to them what they do to you. If they hurt you you would hurt them. It doesn't make sense. In place of revenge, corrective action would be more effective. Revenge is no way to solve a problem.

5. To lie when there are better ways of problem-solving may not be justifiable.

6. It may or may not be justifiable to lie to the following:

a. children
b. corporations
c. criminals
d. insane persons

It depends on the consequences.

7. Some lie where there is no reason, or other way to communicate. Some regard insane people or irrational people as not genuine people, and so lying to them is not really lying. However, on the definition given earlier, a lie is a lie regardless of who hears it, and regardless of its consequences.

8. We often, and without sufficient evidence, accuse people of lying.

9. We sometimes lie because in our situation we are not allowed to tell the truth. We are punished if we tell what we are really thinking. So we tell people what they want to hear, even if it is false. We say what we are expected to say.

If we were to live in a more honest and understanding society, we would not have to lie as much. Censorship, indoctrination, taboos, lack of freedom of expression, promote lying.

10. We lie to avoid telling information which is private. But we need not lie to do that. We can merely say: (a) "I am not free to talk about it," (b) "I would rather not say," (c) "That is a private matter, I'm afraid," (d) "It would be better if I did not tell you," or simply, (e) "Please do not ask."

11. Even social lies may not be justifiable, because we can find polite ways to reply without lying. Instead of saying "I am busy tonight," give the real reason. For example, "Although I like you, I would just like to relax at home tonight and read."

Exercise: Practice replacing lies with polite, true and honest statements.

Strictly speaking, we usually do not have a contract with people not to lie. It is just implied or assumed that we will not lie. Sometimes there are written and verbal contracts which require that the information given be true.

In summary, we tell harmful lies out of ignorance or inability to find honest ways of responding. Such lies are usually self-defeating or contradictory. But this means that even a person who tells a harmful lie need not be blamed. If he or she knew any better, such a lie would not have been told. The Greek philosopher Socrates said that we only do harmful acts out of ignorance. This seems true even by definition. To do harm is to do something that we think is bad and so should not be done.

Also, to tell a liar he or she is bad, says nothing. "Bad" in itself is a vague term. Instead of blaming the liar we need only point out how harmful lying works, and what its consequences are. Instead of blaming the liar, we may help the liar to understand. Blaming "bakes no bread."

In the well-known story, **Pinocchio,** there is a puppet who lies out of ignorance or immaturity, before turning into an honest, live person.

And it was self-defeating for the puppet to lie. The story goes:

> The puppet had scarcely told the lie when his nose grew at once two fingers longer... At this third lie his nose grew to such an extraordinary length that poor Pinocchio could not move in any direction.

On the other hand, if a helpful lie is told we need not feel guilty (feel "bad"). We may praise a doctor who lied to obtain medicine quickly to save a number of lives. Perhaps, then, one's nose would even become smaller.

XI. Ways to Avoid Lying

1. Qualify promises or do not make them at all. For example, "I will try to see you on Sunday," instead of "I will see you on Sunday," or "I will see you if everything goes as planned," or "I may see you then."

2. Make friends with people you can be honest with.

3. Replace harmful lies with honest statements. That is, look for alternatives to lying.

4. Discuss the issue with a friend in order to find ways to solve problems without lying.

5. Be as fair, critical and rational as possible.

6. Work for a society which is more fair and rational, so that truth may be more acceptable. We

can be more honest with rational people and where rules and punishments are intelligent and fair.

If we decide not to tell a harmful lie, we will find we will be more careful in our behavior. If I know I have to tell my friend everything, I will tend not to do certain things which he or she may not like.

Honesty helps us to accept the reality about ourselves and others. It helps us learn how we actually think, and it makes our discussions more significant and interesting. If we can speak with our parents, teachers and others honestly and openly, we can understand each other better and become better friends. It allows us to be full human beings and to achieve our full potentials. We need not look back and say, for example, "I wish I could have really talked with my parents. They never really knew me, and I did not really know them."

It is not easy to be honest, especially because others so often punish us for it. It requires careful handling and planning. Few people are able to accept "the truth" about everything.

XII. Tests for Lying

> "There's one way to find out if a man is honest—ask him. If he says, "Yes," you know he is crooked." Groucho Marx

It was argued that part of the blame for lying rests on the one who believes the lie. We hear the question, "Would I lie to you?" The answer is sometimes, "Yes." How can we tell if someone is lying? Here are some tests, but they are not always certain ones. Some tests are only hints, others are solid proofs.

1. The person admits to a lie. A good test, but one may even lie about lying.

2. The facts contradict what the liar says.

3. The liar is caught in a contradiction of two or more of her or his own statements.

4. We cross-examine the liar to look for inconsistencies. Care is needed here because:

(a) people may change a belief from one time to another.

(b) they require strict, full evidence for some beliefs, but no evidence at all for other beliefs. That is, they may be inconsistent, yet not lie.

Three types of contradiction to look for are:

i. Contradiction by definition (analytic contradiction). If someone says bachelors are married, it is contradictory to the meaning of the word "bachelor."

ii. A statement may contradict our experience, a fact or an action (synthetic contradiction). For example, we claim to be wealthy when we are not.

iii. Inconsistency or incongruity of behavior or thinking. In law, this is sometimes referred to as one's "track record." If you have seldom, if ever, told a harmful lie it will make it easier for you to defend yourself if you are accused of lying. In Aesop's fable the moral given was "A liar will not be believed even when he or she speaks the truth."

We usually follow certain patterns of behavior every day. Police officers look for deviation from these routines to see if anything is out of the ordinary. Similarly, each individual has her or his own thoughts and ways of expressing them. When they begin to change or become different it may be a clue to lying.

If, however, someone is often inconsistent, it is less evidence for a lie. We may cross-examine or question the liar at different times and by different people to see if their story changes, is inconsistent, or contradictory.

The more we know about a person and the way they think, the better we will be able to tell if they are lying or not. The method here, then, is to learn as much as possible about the liar.

5. We find that the liar is not sane.

6. Look for a good reason or motive for telling the lie.

7. See if the liar's story is coherent and holds together.

8. See if the liar has held such a belief in the past. Writings, statements and witnesses may provide such information. A member of one's family usually knows the beliefs one held.

9. Nervousness. This need not give solid evidence.

10. Lie-detector tests. These are not too reliable at present, but may encourage confession

especially when the subject believes they are reliable.

11. Give"truth serum."

12. Hynosis may reveal whether or not it is a lie.

13. A dying person's last statements are often thought, in law, to be true. Supposedly, a dying person has no further need to lie. Clearly, however, a dying person may lie.

14. In law, a quick, immediate, emotional response to a situation is often regarded as evidence for one's true belief *(res gestae)*. Again, there can be a bit of acting in each of us.

15. We are often caught in a lie because we tend to forget it, or fail to realize all of its connections with other facts. For example, if you now decide to deceive by calling yourself "Harold Knaap," you may fail to turn when someone calls out "Harry." This may give you away.

Exercise:

a. Have a person tell you several lies. Find ways to prove that it is a lie.

b. Tell several lies yourself and have someone try to prove you are lying.

16. If someone lied before, it is a clue that their

present statement may be one also.

17. One can ask that the other person be more honest.

18. The absurdity or falsity of a belief is not proof of lying. In various ages nearly everyone believed what was later shown to be false. Today, most people hold some absurd beliefs, or beliefs for which there is no evidence. If someone holds one unfounded belief she or he may well hold another. We may look for a pattern of faulty thinking. Also, we tend to take on the beliefs of our immediate environment and hold such beliefs all of our lives.

Exercises:

1. (a) Examine critically some of the beliefs in various cultures.
   (b) Talk with people with beliefs different than your own. Ask what evidence there is for these beliefs.
   (c) Examine your own beliefs to see if there is evidence for them.
   (d) Read a scholarly critical account of such beliefs, such as an introduction to philosophy book or look up the topic in the **Encyclopedia of Philosophy** (1967).

2. Does censorship and indoctrination help cause one to hold absurd beliefs?

3. See what clearly unfounded beliefs you have. Then see if you have other similar beliefs.

19. We tend to lie only about certain subjects. We lie especially about small or serious crimes, embarrassing subjects, whatever will result in blame or punishment, whatever will be of benefit to ourselves, things we do not want others to know, etc. Look especially at these subjects for possible cases of lying.

20. People often lie by denying that they said or did something. Here we need only obtain witnesses, the written document, tape-record of the conversation, a photograph of the act, etc. In law, not all of such evidence is allowed, because it may be forged or improperly obtained.

In order to prevent lying, the courts have official records made and witnesses present.

21. Sometimes we guarantee the truth by offering to give up something if we are found to be lying. "If I am lying, I'll give you my new car." Two problems here are: (a) that it may be the sort of lie we can never catch, and (b) even if it is caught we may refuse to give up the car.

22. "Look into the liar's eyes. You can always tell if they are lying. That is why you cannot trust people who wear dark glasses."

These are common myths. Certainly people do not lie just when they have dark glasses on. We do not put on lying glasses. We think that if you do not look someone in the eye, they may be lying. On the other hand, we may merely be nervous because we are being questioned or accused. "Look me in the eye when you say that," is not an acceptable test.

Exercise:

Give characteristics, qualities or appearances which people think show that one is lying. For example, nervousness, looking away, men with long hair, women who wear excessive make-up, shabby clothes, untrimmed beard, uncombed hair, dirty hands, etc. Name other qualities. Do these things really show that a person is a liar?

23. We often find out what one really thinks when we show that we agree with them. This is a way of bringing out genuine belief.

24. Strangeness is not always a good test of lying. Odd beliefs and unusual events do happen. As the English author, G. K. Chesterton put it,

> Truth must necessarily be stranger than fiction; for fiction is the creation of the human mind and therefore congenial to it.

There are cases, such as **Ripley's Believe It or Not,** that if we were told "the truth" we would not believe it.

25. Experiments in psychology are often set up to observe people actually telling a lie. This can also be done in everyday life. There is a risk here of

tempting or encouraging people to lie. This may be called "entrapment" or trapping someone to lie, as is often done in the courtroom.

26. Discuss the suspected lie face-to-face with the liar. People may tend to be more truthful when we look directly at them, than they are by telephone or by mail.

XIII. Circular Statements about Lying

Circular statements. These statements seem to say something, but instead go around and around in meaning.[38]

1. "To lie is a fib," says little new, because "fib" means "lie." "Fib" is merely a synonym of "lie." The sentence reduces to, "To lie is to lie."

Other circular statements are:

2. "To lie is to prevaricate,"

3. "To lie is to be mendacious," or "To lie is to destroy the truth." (Subjective truth.)

If we look up "mendacious" and "prevaricate" we will find they just mean "to lie." We have gone around in a "circle" of meaning. We have just repeated a word with other words with the same meaning.

The following statements made by various writers seem to say something. On analysis, they may be seen to be meaningless, circular statements. They are fallacious or trick statements.

4. "To lie is to be dishonest," or "Lies damage honesty." "Dishonest" sometimes means "to lie."

5. "Selfish lies are bad." Here "selfish" partly means "bad."

6. "It is bad to lie." Here "to lie," on the author's view, partly means "to be bad."

In any case we found that some lies are beneficial.

7. "Lying is not just bad, but wrong." Here, "bad" seems to have the same meaning as "wrong," so it is circular.

8. "A lie is bad because it violates our human dignity." Here "bad" and "dignity" mean about the same thing.

9. "It is wrong to tell a bad lie." "Wrong" and "bad" are synonyms.

10. "Selfish lying is self-defeating." "Selfish" and "self-defeating" both mean "bad." It would reduce to, "Bad lying is bad lying."

11. "A lie is wrong because it may produce a bad effect." This is to say, "A lie is wrong because it produces wrong." But a lie may produce a good effect. Also, the truth may produce a bad effect, and that would not make truth always bad.

12. "By lying we lose our moral being." "Lying" again means "bad" here as does "not moral." It would read, "By being bad, we are not good."

13. "Lying is not good." "Lying" as "bad" means the same thing as "not good."

14. "To lie is to keep a secret." If lying means "not to tell what we really think," lying is always keeping our beliefs hidden or secret. Of course, we can hold private beliefs or keep secrets without lying.

15. "You have a right to lie about things which should be kept private." "Right" and "should" are synonyms, because both are value terms. Also, one form of circularity is: to assume what you are supposed to prove. How do we know something "should" be kept private? The author just assumes it should. This is sometimes called "begging (assuming) the question," or assuming what one is trying to prove.

16. "Lies are just bad." The author here just assumes this is true. It begs the question. It is a circular statement.

17. "Lying is morally wrong." This is doubly circular.

18. "If a lie is bad, then one should not lie." "If a lie is good, one should lie."

19. "A lie is a false statement spoken with intent to deceive." A lie may be a true statement spoken or written with intent not to deceive. (See also #24.) The statement also assumes what it is supposed to prove.

20. "That is a 'real' lie." What would an unreal lie be? Does "real" mean the same as "lie" here?

21. "It is justifiable to lie to those who have no right to the truth." Here "justifiable" means the same as "right," so it is circular.

Exercise I:

Try to construct or find circular statements about lying which:

a. use only a synonym as a definition.
b. assume what is supposed to be proven (begs the question).

Exercise II:

Find circularities in the following statement by an author:

Lying is morally wrong because it is an abuse of the natural ability of communication,

> because it is contrary to man's social nature which requires mutual trust among men, and because it debases the dignity of the human person whose mind is made for truth.
>
> — Fagothey (1972)

22. "A lie violates man's 'natural law.'" This assumes what it should prove, and it is not clear who gave us this natural law or what these so-called laws state.

23. It assumes what it should prove to say, "One should never tell a lie."

24. "He lied because he is a liar." Compare: "He steals because he is a thief." It seems like an explanation, whereas it merely says that one lies because one lied. It is not necessarily true. We may be reformed. "He is a liar who does not lie," need not be a contradiction.

25. "Whether or not you should lie depends on your conscience." This reduces to merely, "Believe what you believe," or "Do what you wish to do." "Conscience" is only statements made to yourself. It is your own beliefs, not a special form of knowledge or criterion of moral judgment.

XIV. Contradictions

The opposite of circularity is contradiction. Three types of contradiction were mentioned in the last section, "Tests for Lying":

a. Contradictory definitions (analytic).

b. Statements contradict fact or our experience (synthetic).

c. Inconsistency or incongruity.

Examples:

1. "Truth is falsity." (Nietzsche) (Type # a, above). It is a paradox that this statement is partly false and partly true.

2. It is inconsistent to feel guilty for telling a completely beneficial lie. We nevertheless often do feel guilty.

3. It is ironic or an inconsistency that we must sometimes lie to protect the truth, or so that the truth will be told.

4. A criminal may think you are a fool if you do not lie to protect yourself, but if you do lie, hate society even more for its deceits. (A "double bind.")

5. If all lies were bad, it would be a contradiction to speak of the good lie. But not all lies are bad. There are even "honest lies."

6. All lies are themselves contradictions of type # b above (synthetic). What is said is contradictory to, or inconsistent with, what is believed.

7. One author wrote, "Lying is bad in itself," or "intrinsically bad." This is inconsistent with intelligibility, reasons, and arguments. To say "Lying is bad in itself," makes no more sense than saying, "Humor is bad in itself," "Words are bad in themselves," or "Pencils are bad in themselves." No reason or support is given.

8. "I pledge to do X (e.g., serve, obey, love, etc. someone) forever." If we die, it is a contradiction (type # b above) to do X forever. Also, circumstances change.

9. If we cannot know or determine the future,

we cannot make certain promises about the future. To do so is incongruous and is also a type #b contradiction. It is a contradiction to say, "I will never in any way ever lie."

10. It is inconsistent to require strict rules of evidence in the courtroom, yet allow the way one looks (demeanor) or an oath, to determine whether or not a witness is lying.

11. It is inconsistent for most people to require strict scientific proof for some of their beliefs, but absolutely no proof at all for other beliefs. Some even hold beliefs for which there is little but contrary evidence. Nietzsche expressed it as follows:

'Faith' means not *wanting* to know what is true.[37]

12. It is incongruous that people often will not believe small lies, but do believe big lies. This is partly because it is falsely believed that no one would dare tell such gigantic and obvious lies. But also because the lies are institutionalized as part of the culture one grows up with.

13. Some people of certain faiths believe that if we say one thing aloud, but another to ourselves, it is not lying. For example, we say in court, "I did not steal the money," but add to ourselves the words "before I was born." This is called the "doctrine of

mental reservation." We reserve or hold back part of the statement. A physician may say "You are a fine patient and will become well soon," but add to herself, "at least I have to tell you this to help you to become better soon." The philosopher, Pascal (1623-1662), long ago argued that "mental reservation" is a form of hypocrisy or contradiction.

14. It is contradictory to ask of a liar, "Are you really telling me the truth this time?"

15. Believing makes things true. This contradicts experience (type # b). But believing may help one's feelings improve.

16. "I am faithful to you in my way." This is a way of saying, "I am not faithful to you except in some ways."

17. Lover: "I'll give you the world and make you happy for the rest of my life." This contradicts experience. No one could do that for another person.

18. Social lies require contradiction. We say we enjoyed a meal when we did not.

19. You say, "Your honor," to a judge you do not believe is honorable.

XV. Additional Fallacies about Lying

A. *Equivocation.* This is to take the wrong meaning of words which have several meanings, in order to mislead. Puns are a form of equivocation.

1. To say that to lie is to tell an untruth, can mean two different things:

(a) that it is not true that what is said is the same as what is believed,

(b) that other people do not think that what is said is true.

A lie may involve an untruth in sense #a but not in sense #b. A lie need not be an objectively untrue statement to be a lie. It must only be untrue from the point of view of your own belief. People erroneously say "It's a lie," even when we say what we honestly believe.

Because of these equivocations most definitions of lying are confused and unacceptable.

2. Similarly, a lie may deceive either (a) as to one's belief, or (b) as to the objective truth of a statement, or both. We have to know which is meant if we are to say a liar intends to deceive.

3. It is equivocation to say, "Tell the truth," when we mean, "Tell what the accepted beliefs are."

4. We often equivocate with double meaning words to try to hide our lies.

5. By lying we may intend to deceive in one sense, but intend to help at the same time.

6. Flattery may be factually false, but emotionally true. It is to say, "I like you."

B. *Appeal to Authority*

1. We need seldom accept any statement on authority. Thus, it is partly a fallacy to believe a lie. That is, to believe a lie is to appeal to authority.

2. It is appeal to authority to say we should absolutely never tell a lie because Kant tells us we should never tell a lie.

C. *You-Also* Lie (*Tu quoque* fallacy)

1. For example, you say, "It is alright for me to tell a 'white lie' because everyone else does." The

fallacy is that just because you (or others) lie does not make it any more right that I lie.

2. "Sure we lie sometimes, but who is perfect?" This is also a "you-also" fallacy.

D. *False Cause Fallacy*

To say he lied because he is a liar is a false cause, or false reason. It is only to say he has lied in the past or tends to lie. He may or may not now be lying.

E. *Taking-Part-for-Whole Fallacy*

1. Because someone tells one lie we assume she or he lies about everything.

2. Because it is wrong to lie sometimes, does not mean it is always wrong to lie.

F. *Naming Fallacy*

It is a fallacy to think a lie or "the truth" are entities or things or sentences. We usually say of a sentence that it is a lie (or true statement). A statement alone cannot be a lie. A lie is a relation of a belief statement and the spoken statement. It is a relationship, not a thing or single statement. Similarly, some writers speak of "the truth" as if it were a thing in itself, an entity, or piece of property.

XVI. Lying as Humor

> The aim of the liar is simply to charm, to delight, to give pleasure. He is the very basis of civilized society.
>
> Oscar Wilde

It is easy to lie. Although some special training and study will help, we find that lying is somewhat natural to us. All we have to do is say what we and others do not believe. If you are age 12, say you are age 15. If you are age 60, say you are age 30. This is the mathematics-of-lying humor.

Humor is created by the thought that there is a mistake, but one which is not thought to be bad or harmful. This, then, produces laughter or good feelings. If the mistake is taken as harmful, it can create anger rather than humor. Humor may be seen here as a way of giving insight into and clarifying the concept of lying. (Shibles 1978)

Obvious lie humor. When we tell an obvious lie, it is humorous partly because it defeats the whole purpose of telling a lie. Lies are usually supposed to be taken as truth. Obvious lie is a lie which is not a lie. The contradiction and deviation can cause humor. It is defeated-expectation also, because we do not expect a lie to be revealed or exposed as it is told.

One interesting thing about an obvious lie is that we can lie as if to escape punishment, but tell the truth by so obviously showing that we are lying. For example, "Your book? I couldn't have taken it. What is it doing in my case anyway?" In this way, we may in fact avoid punishment. Humor may make some lies more acceptable. We lie and tell the truth at the same time. Examples of obvious lies are: "I wrote **Webster's Dictionary**," and "I am 6000 years old." These are sometimes called "blatant lies," as when someone says he did not steal the money while it is sticking out of his pockets.

There is also obvious or "blatant" honesty humor. We may be especially honest where it is least expected. This is also a form of defeated-expectation humor. It can be funny to admit that your class voted you the least likely person to succeed, or that your cat probably has a higher I.Q. than you do. This is also a way to escape from being criticized. Others can hardly upset you by telling you you are unpopular, if you already have stated and agreed to it.

It is honesty humor to say what you are really thinking, instead of covering it up, or pretending. For example, we may speak of "cancer cigarettes," or stated honestly, "I admit that I do not know who or what created the world, or if it was even created. Maybe it was always there."

The following are examples of humor created by the language-game of lying. They are classified by type:

Accident

He tells the truth—but only by accident.

I didn't mean to lie, my tongue slipped.

I wrote twenty books by accident.

In politics, honesty can be an occupational hazard.

Now and again we all say something true, even if by accident.

Ambiguity

"Waiter, there is a fly lying in my soup." Reply: "I'm sorry, it's hard to find an honest fly."

He who never lies, sleeps standing up.

I know a tailor who fabricates all of the time.

Behavioral

Here, let me lift this house up for you.

"I have the best manners in the world," he said while eating pie with his fingers.

Caricature

Those who do not tell the truth about war or gun control may be characterized with a cloud marked "lies" coming from the barrel of a gun.

Circularity

Mendacious people make the best liars.

I only lie so that I will not have to tell the truth.

It is my personal belief that liars cannot be believed.

Truth is the problem. If there were no truth, there would be no such thing as lying.

Lies are truths in disguise.

Tell me what you think of me no matter how good it is. (Assumes what it is supposed to prove)

"If there is a tree in the forest and no one sees it, does it exist?" Reply: "Yes, unless you lied."

Of course, I am telling the truth if I say I am. (Assumes what it is to prove)

Context Deviation

Basically, I am honest. I only lie about one thing—the truth.

Contradiction (See also Liar paradox)

Thank you for stealing my money.

I really enjoyed my stay in this dump.

I'll promise you anything except honesty.

Helen, I love you alone; and you too Mary.

I can resist everything except temptation.

I can stop lying whenever I wish. I stopped twelve times in the last seven days.

I never lie—except on Saturday, Sunday and during the week.

I am really telling you the truth this time.

I promise never to make promises.

I always believe the truth no matter how false.

I'm not sure what love is, but I promise to love you forever.

In German, "under four eyes" *(unter vier Augen)* means privately or among ourselves. One may explore the contradiction in self-lie by saying that a self-lie is a lie told "under two eyes."

Believing makes things true.

Tell me what you really think of me—lie as much as you like.

"Are you asleep?" "Yes."

An honest liar is one who unknowingly tells the truth.

I will tell you the truth that cannot be told.

The truth is that no one would ever set off a nuclear bo . . .

He is not lying. He told me himself that he believes that all communication is impossible.

I am not lying when I tell you that I never tell the truth.

". . . belief in things he does not believe." (Thomas Paine, **The Age of Reason)**

Everything I say is a lie. (Also all-fallacy)

"I don't mind lying, but I hate inaccuracy." (Samuel Butler, **Note-Books**)

I truly believe every lie I tell.

Plato said that all language is misleading. Can we believe him?

I am not lying, I am just not saying what I think is true.

I may be a bit mendacious, but I never lie.

"Klaus Hesse, are you here?" "No."

The most important thing in acting is honesty. Once you can fake that you have it made.

Deviation from Desires, the Familiar, the Ideal, the Practical, Purpose, Rules, Standards

My ideal is to be penniless and have no friends.

Whatever you do, do it well; be the best liar that ever lied.

Exaggeration

I exaggerate when I tell you that I am exaggerating. (Also contradiction)

The fact that I am so objective bothered me for centuries.

The truth is, the fish was two miles long.

I cannot tell a lie. I ate the cherry tree.

Hypocrisy

"I would never lie to you . . ." (to yourself: ". . . except daily.") (Method of "mental reservation")

Impossible or Improbable

My brother walked to the moon yesterday.

Insight

If I knew what a lie was, I would know if I lie or not.

In advertising, we use humor to get around the truth. (Also blatant vice humor)

With beliefs like these, they would do everyone a favor by lying.

Social lying is anti-social. (Also contradiction)

"The aim of my life is honesty in all things, even if it means being politely ignored by all of society." (Source unknown)

Pet store clerk to customer: "My animals make good friends and not one of them ever told a lie." (Also personification)

The reason I lie about my age is just to tell the truth about the way I feel about myself.

"One of the most striking differences between a cat and a lie is that a cat has only nine lives." (Mark Twain, **Pudd'nhead Wilson's Calendar**)

Irony

"He lied." "How rare. I have never known anyone who did that."

"Truth is stranger than fiction." (Mark Twain)

Irrelevance

I'm lying if you believe this.

Metaphor Humor

The reason I lie is so as not to hurt the truth. (Also ambiguity, hypocrisy, value deviation)

I not only broke the window, I broke my promise to fix it. (Also ambiguity and value deviation)

White lies do not bother me. It is the black truth which I fear.

These lies will be O.K. I'll just paint them white.

I didn't lie, I just bent the truth.

Miss the Point Fallacy

"Waiter, there is a fly in my soup." Reply: "How did you know I was an entomologist in disguise?" (Also begs the question)

Reduction to Absurd

One way not to lie is not to believe anything. Another way not to lie is not to say anything.

I have solved the deep riddle of how never to break a promise: Never make one.

Does he lie? Put it this way: He tells white lies, blue lies, green lies, and red lies. The spectrum.

I promise to feed your cat forever.

Reversal

A liar seldom stoops to telling the truth.

I said the opposite of what I believe, and got an "A" in the exam. (Also irony)

"My way of joking is to tell the truth. It's the funniest joke in the world." (George Bernard Shaw)

"Can you trust that politician?" "Put it this way. He will fail any course on lying."

Truths are just lies gone astray.

Air Traveller: "Stewardess, you told me I could sit in first class, and besides there is a fly in my soup." Stewardess: "What is an honest lie between fliers?" (Also, "honest lie" is a contradiction)

Riddle (Faulty questions and/or answers)

Q. How did the patient take his liquid medicine without drinking it?
A: He drank it.
Q: But I thought you said he didn't drink it.
A: I lied.

Q: How do you know when a man lies through his teeth?
A: He does not write it down. (Also context-deviation and insight)

Q: How can you tell a lie when you hear one?
A: The same way you can lie any other time. (Also ambiguity)

Sinking (switch high and low values)

I pledge to love you forever—or at least until next week.

If you always tell the truth it will destroy our social life as we now know it.

Understatement

It is a good car: It goes forward and backward.

Uselessness

"The only form of lying that is absolutely beyond reproach is lying for its own sake." (Oscar Wilde)

Value Deviation (blatant vice)

I only lie when I know I will not get caught.

Book title: How to lie to your best friends to get what you want.

I will not believe a lie unless it is big enough.

Why would *I* have eaten the cookies? The cat must have done it.

Why don't you go to him in a perfectly straightforward way and lie about the whole thing. (Also contradiction)

"Waiter, there is a fly in my soup." Reply: "That is not a fly, but a mere reflection."

It's your fault. If you hadn't found out I was lying, no one would have known.

Stranger: Do you mind if I sit here, I won't smoke.
Traveller: No. Please do.
Stranger: (A few minutes later as he lights a cigarette) Ah, I have only known you a few minutes and already I begin to lie.

I love to lie—one of my favorite things. But I never want anyone to lie to me.

I would lie more, but it is too much trouble. Besides, I can't remember them and so I would contradict myself.

"My job requires total honesty." Perhaps you should take a vacation to Crete." (See Liar paradox.)

"Plato is boring." (Nietzsche, **Twilight of the Idols**)[37]

XVII. The Liar Paradox: A Disguised Joke

> Spare me the details of your achievements in the theory of numbers, and speak in a language which I, an ordinary man, can understand. (Popper 1954, p. 162)

The Liar paradox is based on a certain amount of historical fact. (Martin 1970, 1984; Rüstow 1908) The people of Crete had a reputation of being, among other things, liars. Whether or not they actually lied more than anyone else is an open question. Logicians have, unfortunately, unintentionally condemned a whole people merely for the purposes of presenting a logical puzzle.

Epimenides was a Cretan philosopher of the 7th century B.C. The paradox is as follows:

The Cretan, Epimenides, said, "All Cretans are liars."

The alleged paradox is that by sound reasoning we arrive at the conclusion that if he is lying, he is telling the truth; and if he is telling the truth, he is lying.

Logicians and mathematicians, especially, have been deeply puzzled and disturbed by this paradox. The literature on the subject is vast and increases regularly. Yet the problem remains unsolved. In fact, it becomes worse, because new problems have arisen from it.

The logicians are so threatened by the paradox that they believe that unless it is resolved it will seriously undermine logic, the basis of mathematics, as well as thinking itself. (Martin 1970, Bocheński 1961) There may be nothing left. They will not be able to go on.

> The most secure foundations of science, indeed, of reason itself, seemed to be undermined. (Koyré 1946, p. 344)

Accordingly, the Liar problem is seen as an impending doom and referred to as: paradox, self-refutation, vicious circle (the German word for this means "devil's circle," *Teufelkreis*), self-destructive, "Illocutionary hara-kiri" (illokutionäres Harakiri, Falkenberg 1982, p. 68), contradictions, and insolubilia or problems which cannot be solved.

What is meant by "paradox" here? It derives

from the Greek, *para + dokein,* meaning literally, contrary to thought or opinion. It is something which is contrary to our expectations, and sometimes means "a miracle." Thus, a paradox is a kind of miracle which, in this case, haunts logicians.

Quine (1966) wrote, "The paradoxes . . . bring on the crises in thought." (p. 7) He speaks of the paradox as a "catastrophe," "dangerous"; and it is also thought of as "terrifying." (Koyré 1946, p. 344)

> More than once in history the discovery of paradox has been the occasion for major reconstruction at the foundations of thought. (Quine 1966, p. 3)

The titles of journal articles suggest that the paradox is a kind of ghost which stalks logicians in the night: "Return of The Liar," "A New Epimenides," "Drange's Paradox Lost," "The Revival of 'The Liar,'" "Paradox without Tiers" (a pun), "The Strengthened Liar," etc. (Martin 1970, bibliography) And of course, it kills:

> Traveller, I am Philetas; the argument called the Liar and deep cogitations by night, brought me to death. (Bocheński 1961, p. 131)

Unless Philetas is speaking from the dead, this last statement is also itself a Liar paradox.

A similar meaning of "paradox" is that we are led by supposedly good argument to hold that two contradictory statements are true. This is referred to as "logical paradox."

The paradox is sometimes referred to as an "antinomy." "Antinomy" derives from *anti* + *nomos,* or literally, "anti-law." The Liar antimony is supposedly contrary to the laws of logic or rules of ordinary language. Falkenberg (1982) holds that the Liar lacks the conditions for being a logical paradox or antinomy at all. (pp. 65-70)

The paradox has been approached from two basic and contradictory perspectives:

1. as an analysis of ordinary language, and

2. as a problem in symbolic logic and mathematics.

More work has been done on the problem by the latter group as they have felt more threatened by the problem. They attempt to reduce ordinary language to an ideal and perfectly consistent, error-free, symbolic logic. The Liar problem reveals contradiction and error. So it raises the question of whether or not our everyday language can be adequately reduced to a mathematical symbolic logic. Can there be established a consistent "calculus" of sentences? The Liar paradox blocks the way.

Thus, the solution to the paradox will help us to decide if the ordinary language approach is or is not superior to the approach of the logicians. The fears of the latter may prove to be well-founded. They have two fears:

1. that perhaps the Liar paradox will not be able to be made consistent as required for a logical system, and

2. that perhaps the rich insights in ordinary language cannot as yet be accounted by by logic. Thus, the attack on the logician is both from within as well as from without.

There is an extensive literature in defense of the view that ordinary language is where our reasoning takes place, and that it cannot be reduced to logic without obliterating thought itself. (Rohatyn 1974, Ryle 1960, Dewey 1964, Schiller 1912, 1932, Wittgenstein 1958)

For the ordinary-language philosopher, the paradox is not a serious problem, it is not even a problem at all. The paradox is a category-mistake or error such as is often made in language. It is one misuse among many. And it can be accounted for merely as a language-game we play and one which we often find useful. It need not undermine ordinary language. It is this view which I will defend and expand.

The excessive concern with the paradox is seen as a kind of sickness which results from our being careless with our language. But it is curable. It is not fatal. For Wittgenstein, the purpose of philosophy is itself therapy needed to help us find our way back to the proper use of everyday language:

> Such a contradiction is of interest only because it has tormented people, and because this shows both how tormenting problems can grow out of language, and what kind of things can torment us. (1956, 13, p. 52)

The logicians also spoke of the problem as a disease, but instead of finding the cure in a better understanding of ordinary language they reject it in favor of an artificial logic:

> Tarski construed himself as treating the disease by replacing ordinary discourse with a sanitized, artificial construction. But those interested in natural language have been dissatisfied with this medication. (Burge 1979, p. 169)

A brief point by point analysis will not be given of the paradox. Space will not allow a presentation of the relevant logical and mathematical systems, but they are readily available and enough will be said here to be damaging to them.

> The Cretan, Epimenides, said, "All Cretans are liars." If the statement is true, it is false; and if it is false it is true.

The traditional solutions have been of the following types:

1. *Equivocation.* Use of words like "lie" and "true" in two different senses. For example, "I lie" can mean, I just deviate a small amount from the truth. Equivocation leads to a theory of two different tiers or levels of language, or meta-language theories. On this view, the mistake is caused by equivocation and so is not a contradiction.

2. *Restriction.* The paradox is due largely to the fact that the statement refers to itself. Therefore, a rule is made to exclude self-reference. (Russell, 1903, 1964, theory of types.) Thus, when the Cretan speaks of Cretans being liars, it does not apply to himself. This solution exposes another mistake we can make with language.

One of the problems with this solution is that it unnecessarily eliminates useful self-references within our language. (Popper 1954)

3. *Redefinition of Terms.* If "true" is (a) an exclamation (Wittgenstein 1956, #58, p. 31), (b) nothing, etc., the paradox could be avoided. The error would then be that "true" or "lie," etc. are vague or improperly defined, and that is what causes the contradiction.

One redefinition is to assert that the paradox is not an assertion, but says nothing. It is neither true nor false, but meaningless.

It is interesting to note that although "truth," "statement," etc. have been analyzed and redefined, the terms "lie" and "lying" have gone undefined. Paradoxically, the Liar paradox has given us an analysis of almost everything but what lying is. "Lying" has already been defined here in Chapter II.

4. *Context analysis.* This is to show that the error is caused by confusing different contexts. For example, Epimenides was a Cretan but he lived long after the Cretans he is speaking about. This avoids self-reference.

5. *Purpose or intention.* In addition to the above traditional analyses should be added an analysis of intention. Why is the speaker saying what he is saying? To confuse? To reply to a question? or merely to amuse us? This pragmatic approach to the paradox has been neglected.

If a Cretan says, "All Cretans are liars," to amuse us, the sentence is well and perfectly in order as it is. This is one of the possible and valuable uses of ordinary language, which should not be legislated out of existence. It is this view to which I will especially call attention. We can in this sense accept and enjoy ordinary language as it is.

In summary, the paradox involves contradiction and other mistakes we make with language. Some of the mistakes, such as humor, are not mistakes at all, but important uses of language. This point will gradually be further developed.

Using the above types of solutions a number of further observations and solutions may be made of the paradox. (Let E = Epimenides):

1. Cretans may lie only some of the time. This would be the ordinary meaning. At the time E speaks he could be telling the truth. It is probable that everyone in every society has lied at one time or another.

2. E simply does not mean or intend to apply the statement to himself. It is meant to apply only to other Cretans.

3. E could say, "All Cretans are liars," without meaning it or believing it. He merely utters a sentence. We erroneously assume that if a person utters a sentence, that it must be true or false in some sense. One can also intend to utter a meaningless sentence.

4. The statement commits the "All fallacy." How can one ever produce evidence that everyone is a liar or that all swans are white?

5. E could mean the statement: (a) as a paradox, (b) as not being a paradox, but be aware that it could be one, or (c) as not being a paradox, but be unaware that it could be one.

The last case is the one that can create a fallacy. We thought we were saying one thing, but were saying another.

6. No one would ordinarily, seriously say, "All Cretans are always liars." It would be an improbable, vague and useless statement to make.

7. If Cretans do not always lie we need not have a paradox.

8. To say, "If E is lying, he is telling the truth," does not follow. If he lies then some or all Cretans are not liars. We do not know which ones. This does not show that E is or is not a liar. So we cannot conclude that he is telling the truth by lying.

9. If by "lying" we mean "say other than what we believe," then we can lie even though we say what is objectively true. This would itself create a new Liar paradox: One can lie, yet tell the truth. The paradox turns on the equivocation of objective truth and subjective truth.

10. We can mean many things by, "I always lie."

> He means perhaps something like: 'What he says flickers; or nothing really comes from his heart.' (Wittgenstein 1956 #58, pp. 130-131)

11. "Lie" could mean lying slightly, exaggerating or underestimating. This would lessen or

eliminate the paradox. If E says, "Cretans always lie a little bit," it does not give us a clear paradox. For the paradox to work, there must be absolute truth, absolute lies, etc. The paradox as an absolute logical problem is irrelevant or impractical for everyday understanding.

12. "All Cretans lie" could mean "All Cretans 'lie.'" Other formulations could be:

E says, "'All Cretans lie.'"
E "says," "All Cretans lie."
E says, All Cretans lie.
"E says, 'All Cretans lie.'" etc.

We need not continue. These are the kinds of clarifications which are needed to understand the paradox. They are arrived at not by logic, but by an examination of how our ordinary language works.

It was mentioned that those who have written about the Liar have failed to define "lying." They have assumed that we know. The traditional and common definition is that a lie is an untruth told with intent to deceive. (Old view) (Bok 1978) In opposition to this definition, "lie" may be rather defined as consciously expressing other than what we believe. (New view) (Repeated here from Chapter II for convenience.)

A lie is not the same as making an objectively true or false statement. Consider this case. E says,

"I am asleep," or "I am dead." If E believes these statements he is mistaken, but they are not lies. Being a lie does not depend upon the objective truth or falsity of what is expressed.

On this view, we can utter contradictory statements without lying. E can say, "Circles are square," yet not lie. Similarly, E can truthfully say, "All Cretans are always lying including myself." Self-lie, life-lie and self-deception are relevant problems here.

E can also utter what is true, yet lie. If he thinks he is asleep he can say, "I am awake," yet lie.

Therefore, we can lie by expressing what is objectively true; and we can say what is objectively false, yet tell the truth. A lie depends only on the relationship between what is thought (or said to oneself) and what is expressed.

In the Liar paradox a lie was often treated as an objectively false statement. It is not. Nor does being a lie require that another person is deceived. It is a lie whether or not anyone is deceived. We can deceive people even by telling them the truth. If someone is expected to lie, but instead tells the truth she may deceive by telling the truth.

If by "lie" we mean only "deceive," the Cretans could be great deceivers, yet always tell the truth. If "lying" did require deception, the paradox would not deceive. "All Cretans are always liars" is not believable. On the view that "lying" includes deception, another paradox is created as to how one can deceive oneself by a self-lie.

The following chart may be useful to contrast the old and new definitions. (Repeated from Chapter II for convenience.) Let "T" be a true statement and "F" be a false statement. Disregard for the moment that "true" and "false" are themselves vague terms. The chart contrasts subjective and objective truth. It is a lie only when one expresses other than what is believed, regardless of objective belief.

	Column I	Column II	Column III
Row	Person Believes	Person Says	Objective Belief or What People Believe
1	T	T	T
2	T	T	F
3	T	F	T
4	T	F	F
5	F	T	T
6	F	T	F
7	F	F	T
8	F	F	F

On the new definition that a lie is knowingly saying (Column II) other than what one believes (Column I), the following are lies: Rows 3, 4, 5, 6.

On the old definition that a lie is telling (Column II) an objective untruth (Column III), the following are lies: Rows 2, 3, 6, 7. The failure of the old definition is that in rows 2 and 7, the person is in fact not lying, but is said to lie. (Here you are said to be lying merely because you disagree with others. They, however, may falsely think you are really lying.) In rows 4 and 5 the person actually is lying, but is seen not to be lying. This is often referred to as "telling people what they want to believe." In this way, it is the big lies which may go unnoticed in a society.

In rows 3 and 6, you agree with the common view of truth, and so on both definitions it is a lie. In general, on the old definition, if you disagree with people you are said to lie. Some see as a lie whatever disagrees with one's own personal views.

On another view of lying, some hold that almost any objectively false statement is a lie. (Column III, rows 2, 6) In the courtroom a false statement is sometimes taken as sufficient evidence for a lie, though perjury makes use of the new view of lying as well.

From row 2 we can see that E could utter an objective contradiction, yet not lie.

The paradox contains an ambiguity here. We do not know whether "lie" means: (a) objectively false with or without intention to deceive, (b) expressing other than what one believes, or (c) both.

For example, if E lies, or if the Cretans lie, the situation on the new theory could be that of Column I and II, rows 3, 4, 5, 6, or on the old theory, Column II and III, rows 2, 3, 6, 7. But more confusion is possible. E can lie by the old definition, while the Cretans can lie by the new definition and vice versa, or sometimes by one and sometimes by the other definition.

Let lie^1 = lie (new theory)

Let lie^2 = lie (old theory)

Some possibilities are:

a. E lies^1 in saying, "All Cretans always lie^1."

b. E lies^1 in saying, "All Cretans always lie^2."

c. E lies^2 in saying, "All Cretans always lie^1."

d. E lies^2 in saying, "All Cretans always lie^2."

It could also be that some Cretans lie^1 and others lie^2. And it could be that "I lie (higher level language) when I say I lie (lower level language)."

(b) and (c) above avoid contradiction by equivocation. (a) and (d) could involve some contradiction based on self-reference.

One presumably cannot both lie and not lie at the same time. It is not because we do not want to or do not try hard enough. It is because that is not how the rules of our language work to obtain results. In only a very special circumstance would it be useful to say, "He lies when he lies when he lies . . ." "Lie" cannot just be applied to anything. We cannot without personification say, "The cow lied," or "The lie is happy," or "The tree lied." It is not meaningful ordinarily to say, "I lie when I tell what I think is true." The point is that the full context is needed to determine whether or not any particular statement is true, false, or meaningless.

Some statements apply to themselves and some do not. Lie often does not apply to truth telling in the following ways:

1. "I am telling the truth when I say that I am lying."

2. "I am lying when I say that I am telling the truth."

3. A liar lies in saying that she lies. But this is not unusual. Can't we always create contradictions and misuse language? We can violate rules in any language system.

Other similar self-reflexive statements may be observed:

This statement is upside down.
This statement is false.
Everything I say is false.
I am not identical with myself.
I doubt that I doubt.
I am saying nothing.
I am deceiving myself.
I am not myself.
I do not exist.
Honestly, I'm lying.
Everything is mere appearance.
All language is misleading. (Plato)
I can resist everything except temptation.
It is paradoxical to have two contradictory views of paradox.
It is true that this statement is false.
All is lies.
All statements are circular.
Is the question I am now asking you meaningful or meaningless? (Popper 1954, p. 166)
All statements are self-contradictory.
I swear that I swear falsely.
This statement refers to itself.

A statement may be a contradiction in one context but not in another. We do not want a rule which will blanketly avoid all self-reference. Karl Popper (1954) has written a humorous dialogue showing that self-referring expressions are quite useful in language, and that what is a paradox for the logician is, in ordinary language, no paradox at all. Ordinary language is quite in order as it is.

We do not wish to restrict all self-referring

expressions from our language. But we do wish to know what use contradiction and paradox have in our language, and whether or not they are harmful.

> We might ask: What role can a sentence like, "I always lie" have in human life? And here we can imagine a variety of things. (30, p. 183)

> Is there harm in contradiction . . .? I mean: does it make our language less usable . . .? (#12, p. 51) (Wittgenstein 1956)

The following will attempt to show that and how contradiction is an essential and useful part of our language. There is a close connection between paradox, metaphor and humor. All involve mistakes, deviations and contradictions. And metaphor and humor are important uses of our language.

Metaphor may be defined as juxtaposition or combination of opposites (oxymoron) or unlike things. (Shibles 1971) It is deviation from the: expected, familiar, proper, reasonable, intelligible, useful, believed, correct, rules, desired, possible, ideal, real, honest, etc. For example, "Truth is falsity" (Nietzsche), "Memory is a storehouse of ideas," "Time does not exist as such, but is only change," "Life is a lie," "You are my cup of tea."

Metaphor, like paradox, is literally false or "logically absurd." (Beardsley 1962) Because of this, one must look for other secondary meanings to make sense of it. And we find them. "You are my cup of tea," is literally false, but true in other senses. We can figure them out. Metaphors are an intelligible part of language and they are in order as they are. Hester (1967) referred to this as the "presentational immediacy" of metaphor. Robert Frost (1949) put it this way, "All thinking . . . is metaphorical."

The "logical absurdity" of metaphor creates a tension in our thinking to produce paradox, wonder, surprise, riddle. Cleanth Brooks (1948), for example, pointed out that all metaphor involves paradox, but which is necessary in order for us to express and understand reality. (See also Shibles 1971, p. 397 "Paradox.")

Because literal definitions and theories are not to be had, to take them literally is to commit the "metaphor-to-myth" fallacy. Mathematics and logic are thus merely models or metaphors. An artificial symbolic logic would only be a metaphor—useful in some ways but somewhat paradoxical.

> Socrates: Who are all these mathematicians? Theodorus never mentioned their names.
>
> Theaetetus: Barbarians, Socrates. But they are very able. (Popper 1954, p. 168)

Metaphor, then, is part of our language and science as it is. We understand it, and use it. That we should not misuse metaphor by taking it literally, does not mean that it is not useful. If metaphor goes, language and science go along with it.

The Liar paradox is also "logically absurd." It deviates from rules, intelligibility, the expected, etc. We must then look for another interpretation for what could be meant.

> A veridical paradox packs a surprise, but the surprise quickly dissipates itself as we ponder the proof. (Quine 1966, p. 11)

Taken literally, the paradox comes to nothing.

Humor is also a misuse of language. It may be analyzed as the thought that there is a mistake, but one which is not bad or harmful. This produces laughter and certain emotions. (Shibles 1978)

Humor is a funny thing. And it happens in strange places. When we laugh we are looking into a world where all kinds of unbelievable and unusual things happen. In such a world, bicycles only go backwards, triangles are made of spaghetti, there are peas instead of periods at the end of every sentence, paper has only one side, and ice cream grows on trees. And the funny thing about it is that it is a real world.

Humor, like metaphor, is produced by mistakes, deviations, and combining unlike things. There is, for example, contradiction humor, blatant honesty humor, tall-story (or big lie) humor, exaggeration humor, and paradox humor.

Metaphor is one stance we take toward paradox and contradiction. If we take metaphor literally we create a myth or fallacy. Humor is another stance we can take. We can see contradiction, as contradiction. We can see it as a joke and enjoy it.

How are we to take the Liar paradox? Why would one utter it? It has apparently no intelligible literal use. It consists of mistakes, equivocations, and nonsense. But the Liar paradox does have uses—for example, as a joke.

It is a riddle for us to enjoy. The Barber paradox also is such a riddle: "If a barber shaves all men who do not shave themselves, does he shave himself?" Grelling (1936), who is known for one form of the Liar paradox, wrote, "The paradox of the barber is a joke . . ." (p. 23)

Zeno's paradoxes are also amusing and give insight as well. (Shibles 1971a) Exploration of these paradoxes can create critical understanding of time, space, infinity, etc. This is insight humor. It encourages us to explore our everyday language.

We expect Epimenides' statement to be fully intelligible and to make sense. As we suddenly discover that it contradicts itself, we are surprised. With the proper attitude this creates "defeated expectation" humor. We expected it to be true, yet it surprisingly turns out to be contradictory.

It is amusing to imagine that if it is true, it is false; and if it is false it is true: It is like mirrors which reflect each other "infinitely" as in the Linderhof Castle in Bavaria. One has the feeling of some strange, enjoyable or paradoxical experience, but I think no one has yet disappeared into the glass or escaped into infinity in this way.

In the journal **Analysis** (June 1983) the similar problem was analyzed as to whether when looking at myself in a mirror I am directly facing, I see myself looking at myself. And if so, would I also see myself looking at myself looking at myself, etc.?

The case is similar to the story of the dog with a bone in its mouth who seeing and desiring the reflected bone in the water, drops its bone into the pond. In seeking an ideal logico-mathematical language we can undermine and lose touch with our ordinary language.

The problem is that the logicians have looked at the Liar paradox incorrectly—as if it is supposed to make literal sense. It is not. (Martinich 1980, p.

226) It is, among other things, supposed to be a disguised joke. The average person would not take it so seriously.

> Liar-type sentences may be used in jest, or for some other non-truth-claiming purpose, but if someone seriously wished to *assert* one of them we should have to declare him semantically incompetent . . . . (L. Goldstein 1985, p. 12)

Thus, the Liar paradox does not show the inconsistency of ordinary language. It shows certain inadequacies of logic. (Stroll 1954, p. 225) If the logicians had to improve on their logics to include humor, they would have to invent the Liar paradox all over again.

BIBLIOGRAPHY

Analysis "Problem No. 19" 42(3) (1982) 115. Reply 43(3) (1983) 113-118.

Beardsley, Monroe. "The Metaphorical Twist." *Philosophy and Phenomenological Research* 22(1962) 293-307.

Bocheński, I.M. *A History of Formal Logic* trans. I. Thomas. University of Notre Dame Press 1961, esp. pp. 130-133, 239-250, 554.

Bok, Sissela. *Lying: Moral Choice in Public and Private Life* New York: Pantheon 1978.

Brooks, Cleanth, Jr. "The Language of Paradox." *The Language of Poetry* Princeton University Press 1948.

Burge, Tyler. "Semantical Paradox." *Journal of Philosophy* 76(14) (1979) 169ff.

Buridan, John. *Sophisms of Meaning and Truth* T. Scott, ed. New York: Meredith 1966, Ch. 8, "Insolubles."

Dewey, John. *Logic: The Theory of Inquiry.* New York: Holt, Rinehart and Winston 1964 (1938).

Falkenberg, Gabriel. *Lügen* Tübingen: Niemeyer 1982. Sect. 19

Frost, Robert. *Selected Prose of Robert Frost* New York: Holt, Rinehart and Winston 1949, esp. "Education by Metaphor."

Goldstein, Laurence. "The Paradox of the Liar—A Case of Mistaken Identity." *Analysis* 45(1985) p. 12.

Grelling, Kurt. "The Logical Paradoxes." *Mind* 45(1936) 481-486.

Herzberger, Hans. "Naive Semantics and the Liar Pardox." *Journal of Philosophy* 79(9) (Sept. 1982) 479-497.

Hester, Marcus. *The Meaning of Poetic Metaphor; An Analysis in the Light of Wittgenstein's Claim that Meaning is Use* The Hague: Mouton 1967.

Jourdain, P.E.B. "*Tales with Philosophical Morals.*" *The Open Court* 27(1913) 310-315.

Kneale, William and Mary. *The Development of Logic* Oxford: Clarendon Press 1962, p. 757 index.

Koyré, Alexandre. "The Liar." *Philosophy and Phenomenological Research* 6 (1946) 344-362.

Martin, R.L. *The Paradox of the Liar* New Haven: Yale 1970.

Martin, R.L. ed., *Recent Essays on Truth and The Liar Paradox* Oxford, 1984.

Martinich, A. "Conversational Maxims and Some Philosophical Problems." *Philosophical Quarterly* 30 (120) (1980) 215-228.

Popper, Karl. "Self-Reference and Meaning in Ordinary Language." *Mind* 63(1954) 162-169.

Quine, W. V. *The Ways of Paradox and Other Essays* New York: Random House 1966, pp. 1-20.

Rescher, Nicholas and Brandom, R. *The Logic of Inconsistency* New Jersey: Rowman & Littlefield 1980.

Rohatyn, Dennis. "Against the Logicians: Some Informed Polemics." *Dialectica* 28(1974) 87-102.

Rüstow, Alexander. *Der Lügner: Theorie, Geschichte und Auflösung* Dissertation: Erlangen 1908. (Leipzig: Teubner 1910.)

Russell, Bertrand. *Logic and Knowledge: Essays 1901-1950* New York: Macmillan 1964, pp. 59ff.

Russell, Bertrand. *The Principles of Mathematics* Cambridge, England 1903.

Ryle, Gilbert. "Formal and Informal Logic." *Dilemmas* Cambridge 1960, pp. 111-129.

Schiller, F. C. S. *Formal Logic* London: Macmillan 1912. (Also *Logic for Use.)*

Schiller, F. C. S. "The Value of Formal Logic." *Mind* 41(1932) 53-71.

Shibles, Warren. "Zeno: How to Become Turtled." *Models of Ancient Greek Philosophy* London: Vision 1971a. See for Zeno's Paradoxes.

Shibles, Warren. *Humor: A Critical Analysis for Young People* Whitewater, WI: The Language Press 1978.

Shibles, Warren. *Metaphor: An Annotated Bibliography and History* Whitewater, WI: The Language Press 1971, p. 392.

Stroll, Avrum. "Is Everyday Language Inconsistent?" *Mind* 63(1954) 219-225.

Wittgenstein, Ludwig. *Philosophical Investigations* Tr. G. E. M. Anscombe 3rd ed. New York: Macmillan 1958 (1953).

Wittgenstein, Ludwig. *Remarks on the Foundations of Mathematics* Oxford: Blackwell 1956.

XVIII. Questionnaire on Lying

1. Are all kinds of lie harmful?

2. Can some lies be beneficial for everyone involved?

3. Would you prefer to be more honest by not telling even social lies or lies to be polite?

4. Does everyone you know tell some kind of lie sometimes?

5. Is lying always wrong?

6. Should you always tell the truth?

7. Would you now wish to know exactly how and when you will die?

8. Have you ever told a very harmful lie?

9. Do you hold very important beliefs for which you have no evidence?

10. Do you often exaggerate?

11. Do you strongly slant what you say or write?

12. Have you lied about your age so as to pay only the children's fare?

13. Would you tell a lie for $10,000, if no one became seriously hurt because of it?

14. Would you tell the same lie for ten dollars?

15. Would you tell the same lie for fifty cents?

16. Do you think you could ever tell the whole truth about anything?

17. Can you talk completely honestly about everything with your best friend?

18. Can you be completely honest with your parents about your personal life?

19. Could you be completely honest with your teachers about your beliefs and arguments on the subject being discussed?

20. Did you ever lie merely to agree with someone?

21. If you found a million dollars in a wallet, would you lie to keep the money if you knew no one would know that you had lied?

22. If you knew you could get a genuine college degree for telling a small lie, would you do it?

23. Would you lie for a friend?

24. Would and did you ever lie on an application or similar official form?

25. Have you ever seriously lied about your age?

26. Should you ordinarily ever lie about your age?

27. Do you think that before you tell a lie it should be thoroughly justified?

28. Would you tell a small lie in order to obtain a job you would enjoy?

29. Would you tell a large lie in order to obtain a job you need in order to pay off your bills?

30. Would you lie to keep a friend out of jail if the friend is falsely accused of a crime?

31. Would you like to have total mutual honesty with all people?

Exercise: Construct your own questions to test for views regarding honesty and lying.

Lügenbegriffe (Lie Concepts)

The following allows a comparison between English and German concepts of lying.

ableugnen. Er leugnete die Schuld ab. - deny, disclaim.

albern (ahD ala-wari od. alles Wahr) - talk nonsense.

Angeber - boaster.

anlügen - lie to someone.

Aufschneider - brag, talk big.

auftischen - dish up (e.g., false statements).

dick auftragen - exaggerate, lay it on thick.

Ausflüchte machen - make excuses, use evasions, hedge, lie.

kahle Ausflucht - plain or incomplete lie.

einen Bären aufbinden - to tell someone a tall story.

barmherzige Lüge - charitable lie.

belügen - lie, deceive someone by lying.

Betrug (Betrügereien) - fraud, swindle

betrügen - cheat, swindle, deceive.

Bierbankpolitiker - armchair politician.

blanke Worte - sheer or empty words.

blaue Märchen erzählen - tell tall stories.

blauen Dunst vormachen - (colloq.) hoodwink, bamboozle.

Dienstlüge - lies of duty, official lies.

Doktor Eisenbart - (colloq.) a kill or cure doctor, a quack.

dreiste Lüge - a brazen lie.

Ehrenlüge - lie for honor.

erlügen - make something up, fabricate.

Erlügner - one who fabricates.

fabeln - invent a story or fable, fabricate.

fabrizieren - fabricate (excuses, etc.).

fälschen - fake, forge, counterfeit, falsify, adulterate.

Falschheit - duplicity, deceitfulness, two-faced, falsity.

faule Fische/Ausflüchte - bad excuses.

faustdicke Lüge - a great lie, a whopper.

feige Lüge - cowardly lie.

Fiktion als Lüge - fiction as lie.

Flause - fib, nonsense, whim.

Flunkerei/flunkern - fib, tell stories.

freche Lüge - audacious, brazen, bold lie.

fromme Lüge/frommer Betrug - white lie/pious fraud.

Garn spinnen - to spin a yarn, tell a tall story.

Geflunker - (colloq.) fibbing, lying, boasting.

gemeiner Lügner - (colloq.) rotten liar.

gestehen - confess, admit to something.

Gewebe von Lügen - web of lies.

glatte Lüge - a flat lie.

gläubig - credulous, gullible, unsuspecting.

handfeste Lüge - downright or whopping lie.

handgreifliche Lüge - patent lie.

sich herauslügen - to lie oneself out of something.

Heuchelei/Vortäuschung - hypocrisy, insincerity/false pretenses.

innere Vorbehalt (geheimer Vorbehalt) - mental reservation, holding back part of truth.

Ironie - saying opposite of what is believed, irony.

Jägerlatein - tall stories, esp., of a hunter.

kaspern - clown, play the fool.

Kinderlügen - children's lies.

kohlen - (colloq.) tell fibs, kid, talk rubbish.

konventionelle Lüge - conventionally accepted lie.

Lebenslüge -life-lie (see chapter on life-lie).

leugnen. Er leugnete den Diebstahl. vgl. Er leugnet das Dasein Gottes - deny, contest the truth of.

Lug und Trug - lying and cheating, fraud and falsehood.

Lüge als Sprachspiel. (Wittgenstein, L. *PI* 249.) Lie as a language-game.

Lügendichtung - literature composed of tall stories.

lüg/en/enhaft/enhaftigkeit/ner/nerin - lie, invent, fabricate, storytelling/lying/dishonest/dishonesty/liar/(woman) liar.

sich heraus lügen - lie oneself out of trouble.

Lügenbande - gang of habitual, casual liars.

Lügenbericht - false report.

Lügenbeutel - (colloq.) habitual liar.

Lügenblatt - (colloq.) newspaper propaganda.

Lügenbold - (colloq.) habitual liar, storyteller.

Lügenfeldzug - lying campaign against a person or thing.

Lügenflut/Flut von Lügen - flood of lies.

Lügengebäude - edifice or complex of lies.

Lügengeschichte/-meldung - fantastic tales/report.

Lügengewebe/Lügengespinst/Lügennetz - web of lies/spinning of lies.

Lügenhetze - a smear campaign, to devaluate.

Lügenkampagne - lying campaign.

Lügenmärchen - tall story, fiction.

Lügenmaul - (colloq.) impudent liar; one who often tells thick lies.

Lügenmotive - impulses or incentives to lie.

Lügenparole - password, lying words.

Lügenpeter - habitual liar.

Lügenpropaganda - mendacious propaganda.

Lügensack - coarse liar.

Lügensucht - pathological lying.

Lügerei - constant lies, lies.

Massenlüge - lies of the masses, great lies. *(die urteillose, namenlose Masse:* the uncritical masses.)

mogeln - (colloq.) cheat.

Münchhauseniade (münchhausisch) - impossible or tall tale.

Notlüge (meiner Meinung nach ist die Notlüge nicht nötig.) necessary lie, emergency lie.

Nutzlüge - advantageous lie.

offen gestanden - frankly speaking.

pathologische Lüge - pathological liar.

Pflanz reißen/angeben/Pflanzreißer/Pflanzmajor - lie, swindle.

pflanzen (dialect) - to kid.

plumpe Lüge - tactless, impudent lie.

prahlen/kalter Aufschnitt/Prahlerei - brag.

Prozeßlüge - trial lie, legal lie.

Pseudologia phantastica - pathological, extravagant lying, often temporary.

qualifizierte Lüge - qualified lie.

Qualm machen - smoke-screen an issue.

raffinierte Lüge - subtle lie.

du rauchst - brag, say unbelievable things.

saloppes Lügen - (colloq.) casual or careless lie.

Schadenlüge - harmful lie.

Scheinlüge - make-believe lie, apparent or pretense lie.

Scherzlüge - joking or humorous lie.

Schmäh machen - to libel or slander.

schmutziges Lügen - sordid or filthy lie.

schummeln - (colloq.) swindle.

Schwindelmeier - swindler.

schwindeln - tell a "white" lie, fib, cheat.

Selbstbetrug/Selbsttäuschung - self-deception.

Selbstlüge - self-lie. (See chapter on self-lie.)

soziale Lüge - social lie.

Tabulüge - taboo-lie, forbidden lie.

täuschen - disappoint, lead astray; deceive oneself. (Compare self-lie) (sich täuschen)

täuschen/Täuschung/Täuschungsabsicht/Täuschungsversuch - deception, delusion, illusion, error, fallacy, fraud, hoax.

Tierlüge - animal lie.

trügen - deceive, mislead.

Tuerei - make-believe, dissembling, lip-service.

übertreiben/zuviel - exaggerate.

untertreiben/ understatement/*zuwenig* - understate.

unverschämte Lüge - barefaced lie.

Usancelüge - customary lie.

verleugnen - be untrue to oneself, give a wrong impression of, deny.

Verleumdung - slander, accuse wrongly, libel.

Verlogenheit/verlogen - habitual lying, mendacity.

verzeihliche Lüge - excusable lie.

vorflunkern - (colloq.) tell a fib to.

vorlügen - tell lies.

mit Vorsatz lügen/vorsätzliche Lüge/ in betrügischer Absicht - deliberately/deliberate lie/with intent to defraud.

es ihm vorschwindeln - try to make him believe it, tell him lies about it.

vortäuschen - feign, simulate.

Wind machen - (colloq.) talk hot air.

Wortbruch - breach of faith, treachery.

Wortverdrehung - equivocation, distortion of the meaning.

Zwecklüge - purposive, useful lie.

Zweideutigkeit - ambiguous, equivocal.

NOTES

[1]„Das Lügen ist ein Sprachspiel, das gelernt sein will, wie jedes andre."

[2]S. Bok (1978), views of Bentham and Sidgwick are presented in appendix.

[3]A convenient summary of traditional views on lying is in Bok (1978), appendix. (German edition: S. Bok, *Lügen* Rowohlt 1980.) Also see G. Müller 1962; and Lipmann 1927, pp. 152-157.

[4]„Alle aber lehren die gänzliche Unerlaubtheit der Lüge im allgemeinen wie auch die der Notlüge im besonderen. Nicht einmal zur Errettung des leiblichen Lebens ist sie gestattet." (G. Müller S. 338)

[5]„Propagandalügen gibt es überall und zu jeder Zeit." (Becker S. 21)

[6]Becker, p. 9. „Der Begriff der Lüge ist nicht deutlich." (Becker S. 9)

[7]lügen/Lüge: Definitionen

"Lying is not just the assertion of something false: it is a matter of speaking that conceals and knows it." (Hans-Georg Gadamer, *Kleine Schriften* "Semantics and Hermeneutics" (1972) in *Philosophical Hermeneutics*. p. 91).

Lüge: bewußt falsche, auf Täuschung angelegte Aussage; absichtlich, wissentlich geäußerte Unwahrheit. (*Duden: Das große Wörterbuch der deutschen Sprache* Bd. 4, S. 1706)

lügen: bewußt and absichtsvoll die Unwahrheit sagen. (*Duden* ib. S. 1707)

lügen: die Unwahrheit sagen.

Lüge: bewußt falsche Aussage. (*Deutsches Wörterbuch* Lutz Mackensen, 1983)

Lüge: bewußt falsche Aussage oder unwahre Behauptung (im Ggs. zum Irrtum). *(Meyers Enzyklopädisches Lexikon* Bibl. Inst. 1975, Bd. 15)

Lüge: eine bewußt falsche, auf Täuschung berechnete Aussage; sie liegt auch dann vor,wenn Tatsachen mit Absicht verschwiegen oder gefärbt werden. *(Brockhaus Enzyklopädie* 1969, Bd. 7)

Lüge ist die bewußte unwahre Aussage, die in der Regel die Täuschung des Nächsten zur Folge hat. Alle Formen der Lüge (Scherz-, Not- and Schadenlüge) sind innerlich und ausnahmslos unerlaubt, weil gegen Treu und Glauben in der Gemeinschaft festsetzbar ist. [vgl. Kant] (*Philosophisches Wörterbuch* Walter Brugger, Freiburg: Herder 1976, S 230)

Die Lüge ist offensichtlich eine unwahre mit dem Willen zu Täuschung vorgebrachte Aussage. (Augustinus) (*Historisches Wörterbuch der Philosophie* J. Ritter & K. Gründer, Basel/Stuttgart: Schwabe 1980, Bd. 5, S. 535)

Lüge: bewußt falsche Aussage zur Täuschung anderer.

lügen: wissentlich eine falsche Aussage machen, die Unwahrheit sagen. (*Wörterbuch der Deutschen Gegenwartssprache* R. Klappenbach & Wolfgang Steinitz, Berlin: Akademie Verlag 1969)

Lüge: absichtl. falsche Aussage, Aussage zur bewußten Täuschung anderer.

lügen: das Gegenteil der Wahrheit sagen, absichtlich Unwahres sagen, um andere zu täuschen. (Wahrig *Deutsches Wörterbuch* 1968)

[(bem.) lügen: vorsichtig, aber aufmerksam, *scharf* nach etw., jmdm. *spähen*. Der Begriff ist interessant in bezug auf „lügen".]

„Lügen sind personal, sozial, temporal, intentional, verbal." (Falkenberg 1982 S. 14, 15) cf. Note 9.

"To lie is to entertain an untruthful proposition. . . with the intention of inducing another into error." (Eck 1970 (1965) p. 38)

„Lügen sind intentional." „Es gibt keine unabsichtlichen Lügen." (z. B. zu täuschen) (Falkenberg 1982, S. 14, 15) (cf. Note 9)

„Lüge ist die absichtliche Täuschung des Andern." (S. 140) Lipmann 1927 (Görland)

[8]„Sprechmaske" Müller S. 308.

[9]„Von Lüge spricht man dann, wenn das äußere Verhalten eines vernunftbegabten Wesens bewußt nicht mit seinem Inneren übereinstimmt." . . . „Lüge findet sich überall dort, wo bewußt gegen die eigene Überzeugung gesprochen wird." „Die Lüge besteht formaliter in der *voluntas falsum dicendi.*" „Die traditionelle Definition: *falsa vocis significatio* oder *locutio contra mentem.*" See also pp. 320-321 for those who hold intentional deceit is not an element of a lie, and Aquinas *ST* 2a, 2ae, 110. Aquinas holds that a lie is saying consciously to another, other than what one thinks true. (Müller 1962, S. 262, 263, 265) Falkenberg (1982) defines lying as: A hat zu t gelogen genau dann wenn a) A hat zu t behauptet daß p, b) A glaubte aktiv zu t, daß nicht p.

„Die klassische Theorie der Lüge . . . sieht in ihrer simplen Form folgendermaßen aus.

A hat gelogen
genau dann wenn
a) A hat gesagt . . .
b) A hat gewußt

wobei die Punkte " . . . " in (a) und (b) so auszufüllen sind, daß sich ein Widerspruch ergibt zwischen dem, was gesagt, und dem, was gewußt wurde." (Falkenberg 1982, S. 19) He refers to this as „Die klassische Theorie" and „Die simple Theorie" and opposes it. We, however, have argued here in its favor.

„Das Lügen besteht darin, daβ man weiβ, was die Wahrheit ist, und absichtlich das Falsche sagt." (Waismann 1976, XIV. 9) "Lying consists in knowing what is true and intentionally saying what is false." (1965)

". . . if I lie I say one thing and think another." (Waismann 1965, p. 294)

". . . to tell a lie is not just to make a false statement: it is to make a statement that one knows to be false." A. J. Ayer 1959, Sect. 2.

[10]„Eine Aussage die zur Wirklichkeit in einer objektiven Diskongruenz steht, d.h. der Wirklichkeit objektiv widerspricht eine unwahre Aussage, ist deswegen allein noch keine Lüge." (Becker S. 10)

[11]„. . . Als durchaus unwahre, aber nicht unwahrhaftige Aussagen . . . ." (Becker S. 18)

[12]„Der Sinn der Lüge besteht nicht darin, für wahr auszugeben, was unwahr ist, sondern was man für unwahr hält." (Becker S. 17)

Subjektive Wahrheit: „Wer etwas behauptet (=als wahr hinstellt), was er für unwahr hält, *lügt*." (Weinberger S. 58)

[13]„Lügen sei lediglich ein sittlich indifferenter Akt." (G. Müller S. 271) Aquinas says there can be lies with no intent to deceive.

[14]*Selbstlüge*. (See Mele, Bok 1983, Fingarette, Haight). Kant defines "internal lie" as a lie that makes one contemptible in one's own eyes. *The Elements of Ethics* Ch. 2, Section 9.

[15]"The reality of many an *internal* lie, of which men may be guilty, is easy to set forth; yet to explain its possibility seems more difficult. Since a second person is required whom one intends to deceive, deceiving oneself deliberately seems in itself to contain a contradiction." "This insincerity in one's declarations, practiced against oneself, deserves the strongest censure." (I. Kant, *Metaphysics of Morals* (Elements of Ethics), Ch. 2, sec. 9)

„Die Wirklichkeit mancher inneren Lüge, welche die Menschen sich zu Schulden kommen lassen, zu beweisen, ist leicht, aber ihre Möglichkeit zu erklären, scheint doch schwerer zu sein: weil eine zweite Person dazu erforderlich ist, die man zu hintergehen die Absicht hat, sich selbst aber vorsetzlich zu betrügen eine Widerspruch in sich zu enthalten scheint." „Indessen verdient diese Unlauterkeit in Erklärungen, die man gegen sich selbst verübt, doch die ernstlichste Rüge." (*Metaphysik der Sitten*)

[16]Kant wrote, "One lies when, for instance, he professes a belief in a future world judge though he can really find no such belief within himself." *Metaphysics of Morals* (Elements of Ethics) Ch. 2, sec. 9. „Wenn er z. B. den Glauben an einen künftigen Weltrichter lügt, indem er wirklich keinen solchen in sicht findet. . ." *Metaphysik der Sitten* „Von der Lüge."

[17]Bok (1983) speaks of "self-imposed ignorance." (p. 69) „Das Sich-Sträuben gegen die mögliche Wahrheitserkenntnis . . ." (G. Müller S. 301-302) „Bewußte Selbstäuschung" (K. Lange); *„illusion volontaire"* (Souriau) (Reininger in Lipmann 1927 S. 395.)

[18]„Die Lüge verstößt gegen die Pflichten des Menschen gegen sich selbst.": Sailer, Wanker (G. Müller S. 324)

[19]„Die Sprache ist das bevorzugte Medium der Lüge and damit auch des Selbstbetrugs." (Plack 1976, S. 37)

[20]German, *Lebenslüge;* French, *mensonge vital;* Danish/Norwegian, *livsløgn;* Latin, *mendacium vitae.*

[21]„Wenn sie einem Durchschnittsmenschen seine Lebenslüge nehmen, so bringen sie ihn gleichzeitig um sein Glück." (*Wildente* 5 Akt.)

[22]See S. Bok (1983); *Historisches Wörterbuch* „Lebenslüge"; G. Müller S. 286, 302-303, 308; Becker S. 36-48; Lipmann 1927 S. 256-258.

[23]G. Müller S. 302-303; Bok 1983.

[24]Verschiedene Tatlügen: Verstellung, Heuchelei, Prahlerei, Selbstunterschätzung. (G. Müller S. 286, Bok 1983, Becker S. 36-48.)

[25]G. Müller, S. 308, *Historisches Wörterbuch* „Lebenslüge".

[26](Lebenslüge:) „Er unterscheidet sein Sein nicht mehr von der Rolle, die er spielt, er belügt sich selbst." P. Aron in Lipmann 1927 S. 256.

[27]„Der edelste Zweck wird nicht eine Lüge rechtfertigen." (W. Koppelmann *Kritik des sittlichen Bewußtseins* 1904 S. 84ff.; Lipmann 1927, S. 154)

[28]„Der (platonisch-) kantische formalistische Rigorismus ist abschreckend." E. Laas, *Idealistische und positivistische Ethik* 1882 S. 253ff. Lipmann 1927, S. 155.

[29]„Was aus der Lüge folgt, ist nie gut." J. G. Fichte, *System der Sittenlehre* 1798 S. 371ff.

[30]See also section: Lügenbegriffe. Note #7.

[31]„Meineid (154 *St GB*) ist das vorsätzliche falsche Schwören des Täters vor Gericht . . . ."„Falscheid (163 *St GB*) ist die tatsächlich falsche eidliche Aussage, die der Schwörende für wahr hält. Der F. ist strafbar, wenn der Handelnde fahrlässig falsch schwört (z.B. wenn der Täter die Unwahrheit seiner Angaben nicht kennt, obwohl er sie kennen könnte und müßte." (Köbler S. 189, 93) (*St GB* 163)

„Für den subjektiven Tatbestand ist Vorsatz erforderlich; bedingter Vorsatz genügt." *(Strafgesetzbuch Kommentar* #154, 13).

„In Ausnahmefällen kann ein Meineid durch Notstand entschuldigt sein." (*Strafgesetzbuch Kommentar* #154, 13, 14; s.a. 1, 2, 3) s.a. Lipmann 1927, S. 171-186.

[32]„Wenn ein Eid nur subjektiv mein, objektiv aber rein sei, liege Mangel am Tatbestand des Meineids vor.“ (Becker (Frank zit.) S. 59)

[33]G. Müller S. 308-309.

[34]*American Psychiatric Association Diagnostic and Statistical Manual.* DSM III 1980, lying as a factitious (faking) disorder.

[35]See *Diagnostic and Statistical Manual of Mental Disorders* in bibliography. See also Eck 1970, pp. 101-129.

[36]Stuss, D. et al. "An Extraordinary Form of Confabulation" *Neurology* 28 (Nov. 1978) 1166-1172.

[37]Ich nenne Lüge Etwas nicht sehn wollen, das man sieht . . . Die gewöhnlichste Lüge ist die, mit der man sich selbst belügt. (*Antichrist* #55)

„Glaube“ heißt Nicht-wissen-wollen, was wahr ist. (*Antichrist* #52)

Aber inmitten dieser *rerum corcordia discors* und der ganzen wunderwollen Ungewißheit und Vieldeutigkeit des Daseins stehen and nicht fragen, nicht zittern vor Begierde und Lust des Fragens . . . das ist es, was ich als verächtlich empfinde . . . .(*Die Fröhliche Wissenschaft* Erstes Buch, #2)

Plato ist langweilig. (*Götzen-Dämmerung* „Was ich den Alten verdanke“ #2)

Aber der schlimmste Feind, dem du begegnen kannst, wirst du immer dir selber sein: du selber lauerst dir auf in Höhlen und Wäldern. (*Also Sprach Zarathustra* I, „Vom Wege der Schaffenden“)

Ich bin das, was sich immer selber überwinden muß . (*Also Sprach Zarathustra* II „Von der Selbstüberwindung“)

[38]See Shibles, W. "Are All Statements Circular?" *Philosophical Pictures* 1972.

Other examples are: Die Lüge verletzt die „*honestas virtutis*": Thomas Aquinas (G. Müller S. 324)

Die Lüge ist Untreue gegen das ewige Gesetz der Wahrheit : Hirscher (G. Müller S. 134)

Argumente gegen die Lüge weil das Vertrauen verletzt wird: Spinoza; N. Hartmann. (G. Müller S. 329)

BIBLIOGRAPHY

Anscombe, G. E. M. "Pretending." *Proceedings of the Aristotelian Society* Supp. 32 (1958) 279-294.

Ayer, A. J. "Privacy." *Proceedings of the British Academy* 45(1959) 43-65.

Ayer, A. J. *The Revolution in Philosophy* London: Macmillan 1965 (c. 1955).

Barthes, R. in *The Structuralists: From Marx to Lévi-Strauss.* R. & F. DeGeorge, eds. New York: Doubleday 1972.

Becker, W. G. *Der Tatbestand der Lüge* 1948 (S. Bibliographie).

Bentham, Jeremy. *An Introduction to the Principles of Morals and Legislation* Ch. 16, Section 24. London: Athlone 1970.

Bok, Sissela. *Lying: Moral Choice in Public and Private Life* New York: Random House 1978. (S. Bok, *Lügen* Rowohlt 1980)

Bok, Sissela, *Secrets: On the Ethics of Concealment and Revelation* New York: Vintage Books 1983 esp. Ch. III, 5 "Secrecy and Self-Deception."

Bonhoeffer, D. *Ethics* New York: Macmillan 1964.

Christie, R. and Geis, F., eds. *Studies in Machiavellianism* New York: Academic Press 1970.

Cornforth, Maurice. *The Theory of Knowledge* New York: International Publishers 1963.

Davidson, Donald. "What Metaphors Mean." in Sheldon Sacks, *On Metaphor* University of Chicago Press 1979.

Dewey, John. "Knowledge and Speech Reaction." *Journal of Philosophy* 19 (1922) 561-570.

Dewey, John. *A Common Faith* New Haven: Yale 1934.

Diagnostic and Statistical Manual of Mental Disorders (3rd edition) DSM III. Washington, D.C.: American Psychiatric Assoc. 1980.

Dromard, G. *Les mensonges de la vie intérieure* Paris 1910.

Duprat, G. L. *Le mensonge* Paris 1903.

Eck, M. *Mensonge et vérité* Paris 1965. (*Lies and Truth* New York: Macmillan 1970.)

Ellis, Albert and Grieger, Russell. *Handbook of Rational-Emotive Therapy* New York: Springer 1977. *(Praxis der rational-emotiven Therapie* übersetzt von Wolfgang Stifter. München: Urban & Schwarzenberg 1979)

Ellis, Albert. *Reason and Emotion in Psychotherapy* Secaucus, N.J.: Citadel Press 1962. (*Die rational-emotive Therapie: Das innere Selbstgespräch bei seelischen Problemen und seine Veränderung* München: Pfeiffer 1982.)

Encyclopedia of Philosophy Paul Edwards, ed., 8 volumes. New York: Collier Macmillan 1967.

Fagothey, Austin. *Right and Reason: Ethics in Theory and Practice* St. Louis: Mosby 1972.

Falkenberg, Gabriel. *Ansätze zu einer Theorie der Lüge* Dissertation. Universität Düsseldorf 1978.

Falkenberg, Gabriel, "Insincerity and Disloyalty" Society for Applied Linguistics, Duisburg, Sept. 1983.

Falkenberg, Gabriel. *Lügen: Grundzüge einer Theorie sprachlicher Täuschung* Tübingen: Max Niemeyer 1982, S. Bibliographie.

Falkenberg, Gabriel. "Lying and Truthfulness." In R. Haller, ed. *Language, Logic and Philosophy* Vienna 1980a, pp. 328-31.

Falkenberg, Gabriel. „'Sie Lügner!' Beobachtungen zum Vorwurf der Lüge." In G. Tschauder & E. Weigand (Hg.) *Perspektive: textextern* Tübingen 1980b, S. 51-61.

Fingarette, Herbert. *Self-Deception* London 1969.

Haight, M. R. *A Study in Self-Deception* New Jersey: Humanities 1980.

Hartnack, Justus, *Language and Philosophy* The Hague: Mouton 1972.

Häußer, Karl. *Die Lüge in der neueren Ethik* Dissertation. Erlangen 1912.

Hawkins, Peter. "The Truth of Metaphor: The Fine Art of Lying." *Mass. Studies in English* 8(4) (1982) 1-14.

Healy, W. & M. *Pathological Lying, Accusation, and Swindling* New Jersey: Patterson Smith 1969 (1915).

Heinroth, J. C. A. *Die Lüge* Leipzig 1834.

Historisches Wörterbuch der Philosophie J. Ritter und K. Gründer, Basil/Stuttgart: Schwabe 1980, Bd. 5, „Luge", „Lebenslüge" (S. Bibliographie).

Hörmann, K. *Wahrheit und Lüge* Wein/München 1953.

Jakobovits, Julius. *Die Lüge im Urteil der neuesten deutschen Ethiker* Paderborn 1914.

Johnson, Daniel. "Superstition in Economics" *Humanist in Canada* 18 (Spring 1985) 16-19.

Kant, Immanuel. *Lectures on Ethics* tr. L. Infield. New York: Harper Row 1930 (1963).

Kant, Immanuel. *The Metaphysics of Morals* (Part II). New York: Bobbs-Merrill 1964.

Kempson, Ruth. *Semantic Theory* Cambridge University Press 1977.

Kern, A. *Die Lüge* Graz 1930.

Köbler, Gerhard. *Juristisches Wörterbuch* München: Verlag Franz Vahlen 1983.

Küppers, L. *Psychologische Untersuchungen über die Lüge* Dissertation. Universität München 1928.

Kurtz, Paul. *Exhuberance* Buffalo, New York: Prometheus Press 1977.

Lipmann, Otto and Plaut, Paul, eds. *Die Lüge in psychologischer, philosophischer . . . Betrachtung* Leipzig: Verlag von Johann Barth 1927.

Lorenzini, Carlo. *Pinocchio* (Carlo Collodi, pseudonym). PA: Lippincott 1948.

Lyons, John. *Introduction to Theoretical Linguistics* Cambridge 1968.

Martin, M. ed. *Self-Deception and Self-Understanding* KS: Univ. of Kansas Press 1985.

Mele, Alfred. "Self-Deception." *Philosophical Quarterly* 33(133) (1983) 365-377.

Müller, Gregor. *Die Wahrhaftigkeitspflicht und die Problematic der Lüge* Freiburg: Herder (Freiburger Theologische Studien) 1962.

Müller, Max. "The Identity of Language and Thought." *The Open Court* 1(2) (July 21, 1887) 310-313.

Münchhausen, Baron von (The Lying Baron).

Nietzsche, Fr. *Werke* hg. G. Stenzel. 2 Bänden. Salzburg: Bergland Buch.

Observer. "Comments and Queries: Myths Concerning Man." *The Psychological Record* 28(1978) 639-642.

Observer. "Comments and Queries: What Meaning Means in Linguistics." *The Psychological Record* 26(1976) 441-445.

Observer. "Comments and Queries: Words and Their Misuse in Science and Psychology." *The Psychological Record* 31(1981) 599-605.

Pears, David. *Motivated Irrationality* Oxford: Clarendon Press 1984.

Plack, Arno. *Ohne Lüge Leben* Deutsche Verlags Anstalt 1976.

Quine, W. V. "Linguistics and Philosophy" in S. Hook, ed. *Language and Philosophy* New York University Press 1969.

Quine, W. V. *Word and Object* MIT Press 1964.

Quine, W. V. *The Ways of Paradox and Other Essays* New York: Random House 1966. "On Mental Entities" 208-214.

Röhrich, Lutz. *Der Witz* München: DTV 1977. „Der Übertrumpfungs-und Lügenwitz" S. 120.

Rostand, Edmond. *Cyrano de Bergerac* C. Fry, trans. London: Oxford University Press 1975.

Russell, Bertrand. *Unpopular Essays* New York: Simon and Schuster 1950.

Ryle, Gilbert. *Concept of Mind* London: Hutchinson 1949.

Schaar, P. J. v.d. *Dynamik der Pseudologie* München 1964.

Scheffler, Israel. *Beyond the Letter* London: Routledge & Kegan Paul 1979.

Scherleitner, R. *Untersuchungen über den Stil von Wahrheit und Lüge* Dissertation. Universität *Wien 1954.*

Searle, John. *Speech Acts* Cambridge University Press 1969.

Shibles, Warren. *Humor: A Critical Analysis for Young People* The Language Press 1978. See esp. obvious lie, blatant honesty, hypocrisy.

Shibles, Warren. *Metaphor: An Annotated Bibliography and History* The Language Press 1971.

Shibles, Warren. *Philosophical Pictures* Dubuque, Iowa: Kendall-Hunt 1972, pp. 82-102. (*Philosophische Bilder* Bonn: Bouvier 1973, S. 140-174.)

Shibles, Warren. *Wittgenstein, Language and Philosophy* Whitewater, WI: The Language Press 1969. "Intention." (*Wittgenstein, Sprache und Philosophie* Bonn: Bouvier 1973. „Absicht" S. 109-141)

Skinner, B. F. *Verbal Behavior* New York: Appleton-Century Crofts 1957.

Strafgesetzbuch, Kommentar. 21., Auflage. München: C. H. Beck'sche Verlagsbuchhandlung 1982 Sec. 153-165, Seite 1044-1075.

Waismann, F. *The Principles of Linguistic Philosophy* New York: St. Martin's Press 1965, pp. 294-295. (*Logic, Sprache, Philosophie* Stuttgart 1976 #XIV 9)

Webster's Third New International Dictionary MA: Merriam 1981.

Weiler, Gershon. *Mauthner's Critique of Language* Cambridge University Press 1970. (*Beiträge zu einer Kritik der Sprache* 1st ed. S. 176).

Weinberger, Ota. *Rechtslogik* Wien: Springer Verlag 1970.

Weinrich, Harald. *Linguistik der Lüge: Kann Sprache die Gedanken verbergen?* Heidelberg: Verlag Lambert Schneider 1966.

Widmer, Walter. *Lug und Trug: Die schönsten Lügengeschichten der Weltliteratur* Köln 1963.

Wilson, John. *Language and the Pursuit of Truth* Cambridge Univ. Press 1960.

Wilson, John. *Thinking With Concepts* Cambridge University Press 1963.

Winckler, Josef, *Das Lügenjöbken* Emsdetten: Lechte 1981.

Wittgenstein, Ludwig. "Notes for lectures on 'private experience' and 'sense data.' " *Philosophical Review* 77 (1968) 271-320.

Wittgenstein, Ludwig. *Philosophical Investigations* 3rd ed. New New York: Macmillan 1958.

INDEX